Praise for *Sacred*

"*Sacred Anthropology* challenges readers to become active disciples of the word of God whose faith demands a Christ-embodied, radicalized response to inhumane treatment and injustice. This book is for those willing to bear their cross even if they must face isolation, knowing that their suffering will be redemptive within the human plight and predicament. All who are moved by the realities of the current departures from Scripture need to read this work, in which Tyshawn Gardner offers a timely biblical challenge that can only be realized by grace alone through faith alone in Christ alone for the glory of God alone."

—Robert Smith Jr., Charles T. Carter Baptist Chair of Divinity,
Beeson Divinity School at Samford University

"Tyshawn Gardner's book is a must-have handbook for today's prophetic leaders. Drawing from cultural anthropology and the hard-won wisdom of the Black church's struggle for justice, *Sacred Anthropology* provides spiritual, biblical, theological, and practical guidance for preaching, leading, and self-care. I will be using this book with my seminary students, and I highly recommend it for clergy and church leaders addressing social injustice."

—Leah D. Schade, associate professor of preaching and worship,
Lexington Theological Seminary, and author,
Preaching in the Purple Zone: Ministry in the Red-Blue Divide

"*Sacred Anthropology* is the long-awaited answer to many prayers. This book will meet the needs of many who have been hoping and waiting for such a long time for the help it brings."

—J. Alfred Smith Sr., professor emeritus,
Berkeley School of Theology, Berkeley, California

"In this interdisciplinary study, Tyshawn Gardner brings together the mind of an anthropologist, the heart of an advocate for justice, and the soul of a caring preacher to expose and eradicate the root causes of the perennial problems plaguing US society. For those for whom God is the source and summit of every stride to tear down the unjust systems of our times, this is your book. For those who seek to give voice to pain beyond generalities and to offer a brand of prophetic proclamation that is informed by grassroots activism, this is your book. For those who have never welcomed the idea that we can wage a war against physical, structural, and cultural forms of violence by demonizing and deriding those with whom we disagree, this is your book. For those in the pulpit and the pew who are looking for spiritual disciplines that will sustain them in their struggles for justice and thus not let them 'grow weary in well-doing,' this is your book."

—Abraham Smith, professor of New Testament, Perkins
School of Theology, Southern Methodist University

SACRED
ANTHROPOLOGY

SACRED ANTHROPOLOGY

Prophetic Radicalism for Pulpit and Pew

Tyshawn Gardner

Fortress Press
Minneapolis

SACRED ANTHROPOLOGY
Prophetic Radicalism for Pulpit and Pew

Cover image: louis moncouyoux / Unsplash.com
Cover design: John Lucas Design

Print ISBN: 978-1-5064-8124-1
eBook ISBN: 978-1-5064-8125-8

For My Daddy,

Robert Edward Gardner

Exemplar of truth, wisdom, and
the courage to be authentic

Contents

Introduction

Ministry That Opens Doors

And immediately all the doors were opened,
and everyone's bonds were unfastened.
—Acts 16:26

IN JULY 1839, African captives aboard the *Amistad* revolted against the ship's slave-trading crew. The captives, who had been kidnapped from the West African coast of present-day Sierra Leone, killed the captain and cook and seized control of the ship. Later, the newly self-emancipated Africans were apprehended by a US ship that led them to Long Island, New York, where they were jailed to await their fate. With the help of abolitionists, they sued for their freedom and the right to return to Africa. Their case was eventually tried before the United States Supreme Court, where they were represented by former president John Quincy Adams. The court ruled that the Africans were free citizens and must be allowed to return to their homes. Both the actions of the slaves and the advocacy of Adams and others who demanded their freedom were acts of prophetic radicalism. By resisting and revolting against a racist and oppressive system designed to deny freedom to image bearers of ebony hue, their actions opened the door for many others who would be affected by social and racial oppression centuries after this mutiny. This act of rebellion sent a clear message to both slave and slaveholder: human beings were not created to be subjected to dehumanization at the hands of other humans. The *Amistad* mutiny also speaks to the concept of prophetic radicalism by showing that doors of freedom are opened through acts that expose evil, advocate for the oppressed, and disrupt unjust systems—a truism that holds nearly two centuries later.

In 1938, Buell Gallagher, then president of Talladega College, commissioned famed African American painter Hale Aspacio Woodruff to paint three large-scale works depicting the uprising aboard the *Amistad* and the events that followed. The resulting works, known as the Amistad Murals, depict three scenes: *The Revolt, Court Scene*, and *Back to Africa*. These paintings burst with color and are vivid expressions of the spirit of determination that sustained those aboard the *Amistad*. The completed paintings were hung on the walls of the library at Talladega College, where they remained for many years.

When Dr. Billy Hawkins came to take the helm as president of Talladega College in 2008, the school was failing, and its doors were about to be shut for good. Enrollment was at a mere 261 students, and alumni giving was not enough to sustain the school's operations. Trying to save the college, Hawkins thought to have one of Talladega's few assets appraised—the Amistad Murals. Could these murals, painted over seventy years earlier, keep the doors of Talladega College open?

Dr. Hawkins called the High Museum of Art in Atlanta, Georgia, which sent representatives to appraise the paintings. The assessor called Dr. Hawkins and said, "We have good news and bad news." The good news, exclaimed by the High Museum expert, was that "the first painting is worth $20 million, and the other paintings are worth over $20 million!" Then he gave the bad news: "If we don't get them restored now, they won't be worth the wall that they are hanging on."[1] Representatives from the High Museum spent a week carefully, cautiously, and meticulously removing the murals from the walls of the Talladega library. After the paintings were removed and restored, they spent three years traveling around the world, attracting art lovers from every corner of the globe. The act of resistance on the Atlantic Ocean in 1839 that inspired the Amistad Murals in turn produced another act of liberation by keeping the doors of Talladega College open.

The Amistad Murals not only kept the doors of Talladega College open; they also opened other doors. On a cold day in January 2019, I had the opportunity to be present at Talladega College to celebrate the opening of the William R. Harvey Museum of Art, where the Amistad Murals are currently displayed. An hour after the ribbon cutting for the art museum, Talladega College opened the doors to a new forty-five-thousand-square-foot residence hall. A year later, they opened the doors of the Billy C. Hawkins student activity center. Those murals, once off the walls of the library and restored, kept the doors of Talladega College open and were a catalyst that opened more doors of opportunity for students to walk through. One radical act continues to reverberate throughout history.

We live in a time when many doors are closing. The most urgent need in our country today is more open doors. The greatest threat to vulnerable and marginalized communities is the fact that doors are closing. Doors are closing on voting rights, women's economic enfranchisement, and Black and brown immigrants. Doors are closing on quality education. Prison doors are closing, locking up our best and brightest. And yes, church doors are closing! Yet there is good news! This book provides an assessment of the value of prophetic radicalism and seeks to restore it in the church so that it can lead to open doors beyond the walls of the church.

Just as the Amistad Murals' value increased once they moved beyond the walls of Talladega College, prophetic radicalism works best when it moves beyond the walls of the church and the academy. When pastors and congregations take prophetic radicalism into their wider communities, they serve as fierce witnesses, flinging open doors of justice and human advancement with the hope that they will remain open. Prophetic radicalism needs to be restored in the public square, political spaces, the social arena, and fundamentalist religious bases.

This book positions the pastoral office as a center for prophetic radicalism, but prophetic radicalism should not be limited to the pastoral office. Ultimately, the pastor is a member of the congregation; an effective pastor sits at both the center and the margins of congregational life. Just as the body of Christ is a priesthood of all believers, prophetic radicalism is a congregational responsibility that transcends the hierarchical and gender-exclusive boundaries of ministerial responsibility. Pastors who exemplify prophetic radicalism make radical prophetic disciples. Pastors and parishioners who engage in prophetic radicalism possess the potential to open doors beyond those of the church.

I am a son of the Black church, an ecclesial tradition that embodies prophetic radicalism from pulpit to pew. This book unapologetically extracts presuppositions, values, practices, and truths from that tradition. However, just as the Black church does not have a monopoly on prophetic radicalism, this book is intended to be a resource for pastors, congregations, and preachers of any cultural or church tradition.

Prophetic Radicalism: The Work of Christ

Radix, meaning "root," is the Latin etymology of the word *radical*. Radical is defined as "pertaining to the root." Thus, it is usually associated with fundamental aspects. Prophetic radicalism is aimed at addressing the roots or fundamental causes of spiritual and social evil, gender exploitation, sin, and injustice. It is not interested in surface, veneer, or superficial but sincere answers to addressing social evil in our world; rather, the aim is to eradicate evil from the root. The ministry and preaching of Jesus Christ addressed evil in this very way. The redemptive work of Jesus Christ is not only the most fundamental answer to spiritual and social sin; his life and work represent the holistic response to sin, the root cause of evil and injustice. Evil demands a radical response, and the redemptive work of Jesus Christ is radical.

There is an intra-Trinitarian aspect to prophetic radicalism. Prophetic radicalism is God's call to the body of Christ to continue the work of Christ in the power of the Holy Spirit. Prophetic radicalism is a description of the person and work of Jesus Christ. The work that God accomplished through Christ on the cross is nothing short of radical. Jesus is the ultimate prophet. Continuing his ministry in the spirit and nature of the Old Testament prophet, the earthly ministry of Jesus marks him as the obedient, heaven-sent Son of God; chief herald of the kingdom of God; preeminent enemy of Satan, sin, and evil; and exemplar of God's vision for humanity. Jesus was a radical prophet. Thus, he called his disciples to embody this same prophetic radicalism: "Proclaim as you go, saying, 'The kingdom of heaven is at hand.' Heal the sick, raise the dead, cleanse lepers, cast out demons" (Matt 10:7–8; see also Matt 28:16–20; and Luke 10:1–12).

This book locates prophetic radicalism in the person of Jesus Christ and articulates the functionality of prophetic radicalism through a pastoral theology that includes both pastor and congregation. I refer to this in the book as "sacred anthropology." Through the power of the spirit of Christ, the will of God is communicated to the forces of evil, both by proclamation of the Word and through deeds of activism that are anchored in that proclaimed Word. Thus, prophetic radicalism employs the ethics of Christ, which is lived out and embodied in the fruit of the Spirit in order to disarm evil, to address those who have bought into the everyday norms that perpetuate injustice, and to practice resistance for the good of the community.

Arrangement of the Book

Chapter 1 introduces a theology for sacred anthropology. The term *sacred anthropology* will be defined, and the relationship between cultural anthropology and theological anthropology will be examined.

Chapter 2 defines and examines prophetic radicalism. This chapter will explore how Jesus embodies prophetic radicalism through the theocratic offices of priest, prophet, and king. I also place emphasis on the historical pattern of prophetic radicalism in the Black church.

Chapter 3 introduces sacred anthropology as the most necessary component of prophetic radicalism and as a pastoral model to help pastors navigate the complexities of the cultural terrain. The sacred anthropologist interprets three major areas: the Scriptures, the congregation, and the contemporary crises affecting the congregation.

Chapter 4 promotes social crisis preaching as the primary method by which radically prophetic congregations are formed. Social crisis preaching has been present and prominent throughout the history of the Christian church and is an integral component of the pastoral office. People who commit to social crisis preaching engage in Spirit-inspired, Christian proclamation anchored in the revelation of God's word regarding redemptive justice as God's response to social crisis. These pastors and preachers share in the pain of injustice with those who hear their sermons by living incarnationally with their congregations. Social crisis preaching is committed to exposing evil, advocating for the vulnerable, and calling congregations to intentional acts of redemptive disruption. Social crisis preachers aim to reconcile a world filled with injustice to a world where the justice and peace of God are the vision.

Chapter 5 focuses on the spirituality necessary to sustain prophetic radicalism and explores how suffering produces hope and resilience. Drawing from the deep well of African American tradition, this radical spirituality is portable and thus effective in hewing stones of hope from mountains of despair by employing the fruit of the Spirit as a tool for effective resistance.

Chapter 6 delves into the important topic of clergy self-care. Dedicated to pastors, this chapter will identify the causes of weariness that often lead to mistakes and burnout. Considering the increase in dropout and suicide rates among clergy, this chapter will identify the causes of weariness brought on by the toll that social justice activism takes on the mind, body, and family of the pastor. Even the work of justice can become idolatrous. This chapter also offers five spiritual disciplines that will restore the soul of the pastor who is weary from the responsibilities of prophetic radicalism. The pastor must maintain a devotion to God in the pursuit of justice.

As you read this book, I pray that you will develop a fervent desire to commit to the radical prophetic ministry of Christ. Through the power of the Holy Spirit, prophetic radicalism is the key to unlocking the closing doors of equity, justice, and prosperity. Prophetic radicalism is the spiritual response by which the church opens—and keeps open—doors in solidarity with the One who can "open doors that no man can shut."

1

Toward a Theology of Sacred Anthropology

SACRED ANTHROPOLOGY IS a biblical and theological examination of image bearers and their social relationships that employs cultural anthropology to help solve injustice-related crises. *It is the conveyance of a concept that applies prophetic radicalism to understanding the social order so that we can affect a biblically based response designed to call the church to a kingdom focus that holistically addresses humanity.* Sacred anthropology brings theological anthropology and social-scientific (cultural) anthropology together to provide the church with a methodology for dealing prophetically with social injustices in our world. Among the subfields of anthropology—archaeology, linguistics, and physical and cultural (social) anthropology—sacred theology is most akin to cultural anthropology.[1] Tanya Maria Golash-Boza, in her celebrated and notable text *Race and Racisms: A Critical Approach*, surmises, "Before the rise of science, Westerners understood the world primarily in biblical terms. Theology provided explanations for everything."[2] This fundamentalist approach to reading and interpreting the Bible led to a blatant disregard for science and critical approaches to theology. Hence in some cases, adherents held harmful views of humanity, where there stood a sharp dichotomy between the Bible and science. Sacred anthropology uses the Bible, history, science, and cultural awareness as tools for congregations to engage in redemptive prophetic radicalism.

After graduating from Pickens County High School in Reform, Alabama, a small town of about 2,500 people, I began a career in the navy that took me around the world. The Naval Recruit Training Center in San Diego, California, became my first home outside of Alabama. And what a culture shock! In the rural Pickens County of the late 1980s and '90s, most families held conservative social values, and race relations were mostly without incident as long as everyone knew the unwritten rules and stayed in the spaces created for them, especially when it came to romantic relationships between the races.[3] What I witnessed in California was so beyond the small town mentality in which I left Alabama that I wrote to my parents almost daily about the unbelievable sight of interracial couples holding hands and riding together in drop-top convertibles in broad daylight, without experiencing the whispers and sidelong glances of passersby or fearing far worse.

However, ports of call in Egypt, Israel, Turkey, Greece, Spain, Italy, and other places stimulated an admiration and respect of people, their cultures, and their values that still lives in me to this very day. I didn't become nor did I aspire to be an anthropologist, but my desire to understand people, their customs, their values, and their communities has been a major advantage in my preaching and pastoral ministry. It has allowed me to recognize beauty, see honor, appreciate perspectives, and esteem traditions that are drastically different from those responsible for my early development in Pickens County. Most of all, it allowed me to shed any feelings that the image bearers from other nations in God's world were inferior to me or my country.

Sacred anthropologists differ from cultural anthropologists by saturating the insights of cultural anthropology with the sacred truth of the Bible. An anthropologist studies humans and employs those findings to solve human problems. A sacred anthropologist, by developing an awareness of and appreciation for other cultures, communicates God's vision for humanity to fallen people who sometimes harm others in this fallen world. A sacred anthropologist is a tool in the hand of God to lead God's people in this world. Only God can grant insight into the human condition and reveal to us what it means to be truly human (Rom 5); anthropology, however, brings a critical awareness of the world beyond the biblical text to pastors and congregations.

The American Anthropological Association describes its mission as "advancing human understanding and applying this understanding to the world's most pressing problems."[4] For sacred anthropologists, this goal is valid but incomplete. Human understanding is indeed vital for the solutions to the world's most pressing problems. However, human understanding alone is insufficient for world-sized problem-solving. The revelation of God as it exists in Scripture provides the pulpit and pew with knowledge of God's purpose for creation, as well as an understanding of God's redemptive will for all humans to flourish.

Restricting one's efforts toward resolving problems in the world to the use of mere "human understanding and knowledge" places the sole responsibility of human problem-solving on the shoulders of frail and fallen humanity, whose efforts will not last. History has shown that understanding and knowledge of cultures and peoples alone, without the superintending power of the word and spirit of God, has often led to the exploitation, denigration, and destruction of people and civilizations.[5] Humanity, left to its own devices and resources, can manufacture inhumane atrocities, including enslavement, violence against women, the taking of land from Indigenous peoples, civil wars, and the Holocaust, to name just a few. Racist immigration and citizenship policies, such as the Indian Removal Act of 1830, the Naturalization Law of 1790, the 1882 Chinese Exclusion Act, and the Johnson-Reed Act of 1924 are examples of systemic and structural racism that have disenfranchised nonwhite immigrant communities.

The solutions to the most pressing problems in our world will come when we accept the truthful claims of God's word as the epistemological foundation of our understanding of humanity. Applying this Scripture-based understanding is the work of the sacred anthropologist. White, male, western biblical and social presuppositions cannot be imposed as viable solutions for critical and complex social issues that involve women and other ethnicities. In this way, sacred anthropology transcends any nationalistic and cultural claims that seek to trump or subvert God's plan for creation. Like that of the cultural anthropologist, the work of the sacred anthropologist involves the excavation of buried biblical truth (exegesis) and the mining and examination of historical and cultural data (understanding the world of your parishioners). These are employed together to better understand God's people and grant us a greater awareness of all our contributions to God's unfolding story of redemption in Christ.

As an anthropologist probes the earth for clues about ancient civilizations, the preacher, as a sacred anthropologist, must dig and mine for cultural truths out of mountains of misconceptions and layers of lies. Developing the tools to pick apart and break up the fallow, dry, and cold ground of compressed half-truths can be daunting. The broken tools of flawed exegetical practices and racist anthropology, introduced by previous generations of preachers and passed down to us, have proven to be dull, slow, and incapable of removing the underbrush of cultural ignorance and bias.[6] Thus, it is responsible for choking out the fresh growth of justice, harmony, and reconciliation in our churches and communities. By developing these tools, the sacred anthropologist can understand God's people better and is more capable of communicating God's word to a variety of people.

Cultural anthropology is an integral component of sacred anthropology for three primary reasons. Used together with theological anthropology, they *marry prophetic radicalism and the social order for the purpose of affecting a biblically based response designed to call the church to a kingdom focus that holistically addresses humanity.* In chapter 3, we will see how the three reasons below serve as practical steps for pastors and pew to activate sacred anthropology in preaching and ministerial practices.

First, cultural anthropology helps the sacred anthropologist think about race. In the United States, racism has been the most violent and dehumanizing outgrowth of sin. Systemic racism is a reality that Black and brown communities have endured for centuries. It is imperative that the church use all redemptive tools at its disposal to address racism and the devastating grip this sin holds on the church. Historian Malcolm Foley writes, "In the American context, race has been the most oft-used weapon of oppressive war; thus, Christ's church has a particular responsibility to beat that sword into a plowshare and seek to heal the wounds that weaponized racialization has wrought. Battling an enemy like weaponized racialization requires us to use all of the resources we have at hand, whether they be moral reasoning, history, sociology, biblical interpretation, theology, or activism, to see it weakened and defeated."[7]

Renowned scholar Joe R. Feagin describes "'racial oppression' and 'systemic racism' as shorthand terms for the European American oppression of African Americans since the 1600s—even though in the earliest period the African American targets of color-coded oppression were viewed by their oppressors as primarily different in terms of skin color and culture, and not fully in terms of 'race' as biologically conceived."[8] The outworking of systemic racism intentionally devastates communities of color and economically exploits Black and brown individuals through inequitable wealth distribution and exploitive labor laws and practices.[9] Systemic racism also has public health ramifications. Feagin further insists that "systemic racism encompasses a broad range of white-racist dimensions: the racist ideology, attitudes, emotions, habits, actions, and institutions of whites in this society. It is a material, social, and ideological reality that is well-embedded in major U.S. institutions."[10]

The scholarly position of cultural anthropologists holds that race is a social construct and that there is no scientific reason for humanity to be classified based on skin color or physical characteristics. Robert Wald Sussman argues, "There is no inherent relationship between intelligence, law-abidingness, or economic practices and race, just as there is no relationship between nose size, height, blood group, or skin color and any set of complex human behaviors."[11] Gradually and refreshingly, society was confronted with new scientific theories and fresh perspectives that challenged the prevailing racist thoughts in many quarters of the country. Brian Howell and Jenell Williams Paris contend, "Biologically speaking, there is no reason to group people according to hair texture, skin color, or eye shape than by any other biological feature."[12]

Race "was a mode of classification linked specifically to peoples in the colonial situation. It subsumed a growing ideology of inequality devised to rationalize European attitudes and treatment of the conquered and enslaved people."[13] While it is true that the Bible does provide narratives of ethnic conflicts, unless the text under review specifies a particular ethnic group (i.e., Jews and Samaritans or Jews and Moabites), there is no parallel between the historical racial conflicts between African Americans and white Americans and the conflicts among the ethnic groups of the New Testament. J. Daniel Hays writes,

> Traditionally, biblical scholarship has tended to overlook much of the ethnic diversity in the New Testament world. Discussions generally cover the Greco-Roman culture and the Jewish Diaspora, assuming subconsciously that the New Testament world consisted of only two ethnic groups: Jews and Greco-Roman Gentiles. Occasionally the "Barbarians" are included as another group. But there still seems to be an underlying assumption in much of the literature that everyone who was not Jewish or "Barbarian" was "Greco-Roman," as if this were a monolithic ethnic group. However, while there was definitely a Greco-Roman culture, there was not really any Greco-Roman ethnic group.[14]

Martin Bulmer and John Solomos comment, "Although usages of the term 'race' have been traced somewhat earlier in a number of European languages, the development of racial doctrines and ideologies begins to take shape in the late eighteenth century and reached its high point during the nineteenth and early twentieth centuries. This is, of course, not to say that the category of race was not used in earlier times. But it is clear that from towards the end of the eighteenth century the meanings attached to the notion of race begin to change quite significantly."[15] Harriet A. Washington confirms, saying, "Use of the term *race* to denote biologically different types of mankind evolved only in the eighteenth century. . . . This period coincided with the growth of the slave trade, when biological distinctiveness of men became economically important."[16]

Slavery in ancient times and cultures was part of the social milieu. However, in the seventeenth and eighteenth centuries in Europe and the New World, slavery was solely assigned to Africans. Murry J. Harris comments, "In the first century, slaves were not distinguishable from free persons by race, by speech or by clothing. . . . They were not denied the right to public assembly and were not socially segregated. . . . Their natural inferiority was not assumed."[17] Russell G. Moy states, "The social construction of race began with the importation of African slaves to the American colonies in the early seventeenth century. Early colonial history was multicultural from the beginning. Yet slavery as we know it today was the result of a continuing process. There was a gradual deterioration in the status of Africans, from limited indentured servitude to persons who with their descendants, were slaves for life. Thus, the institution of slavery did not suddenly appear, but was a historical development."[18] The correlations between cultural anthropology and theological anthropology are the basic and fundamental teachings on ethnicity and race and their rejection of human hierarchy based on physical characteristics.

The Bible supports the monogenesis theory of creation, which teaches that all of humanity has one Creator (Gen 1–2; Acts 17:26). Cultural anthropology engages ethnographic studies to provide a cultural context from an inside perspective. Sacred anthropology is particularly helpful in assisting congregations to confront social injustice caused by or rooted in racism. Racism was sustained, supported, and spread due to the powerful influence of scientific racism, taught and developed by scientists and anthropologists and adopted by theologians, Christians, and preachers during much of the eighteenth and nineteenth centuries.[19] Many of these scientists and anthropologists, based on their research and writings, supported polygenesis, a theory of human origins that states that the varying races have different origins and different creators.[20] It is befitting that a discussion concerning an understanding of humanity explores the discipline of anthropology, since flawed concepts of anthropology were partly responsible for the racial myths and *mis*understanding of people in America and America's churches.

Sacred anthropology baptizes anthropology in the word of God for biological accuracy and theological clarity.

One of a plethora of reasons why views on race are important to sacred anthropology is that the effects of racism have inhumane consequences to image bearers, thus refuting the biblical claims of the word of God concerning human identity. These inhumane ramifications cause some scholars to contend that racism is embedded in the legal foundations of the United States.[21] Because the church has supported some of these audacious and unbiblical claims, it has been complicit in the creation of unjust and unbiblical systems.[22] It is therefore incumbent on the church to correct this error concerning human identity and to forge a new path forward in our social relationships.

Second, cultural anthropology is interested in the causes of inequality in society. Cultural anthropologists examine social stratification, agency, power, wealth, and race, among other factors, as reasons for inequality. While the Bible points to sin as the root of racism, inequality, and social issues, cultural anthropology exposes and names the structures where sin and evil hide. Sin has a name. Whether it is white supremacy, corporate exploitation, national idolatry, toxic cultural pride, sexism, paternalism, prison industrial complex, drug dealing, religious bigotry, gender inequality, or educational inequity, the sin must be named in order to expose and extract it from the moral fiber of humanity.

In the United States and in churches across the United States, women continue to be overlooked, abused, exploited, and undervalued. Sacred anthropology raises a serious and strong argument in defense of women and advocates for equality for women in the church and in the world in which we live. Since we live in a society where women and their wombs are often politicized by men, the sacred anthropologist confronts paternalistic and political posturing that is often cloaked as moral concern. In the era of slavery, through the horrors of breeding, beating, forced work, medical experimentation, and rape, to name a few, white men have often sought control over Black women's bodies. Angela Davis poignantly argues this point: "If the most violent punishment of men consisted in floggings and mutilations, women were flogged and mutilated, as well as raped. Rape, in fact, was an uncamouflaged expression of the slave holder's economic mastery and the overseer's control over Black women as workers. The special abuses inflicted on women thus facilitated the ruthless economic exploitation of their labor."[23] The lust to control women's bodies has yet to cease, since many states in the country are pushing to enact unjust, immoral, and insensitive reproductive health legislation that would bar women from terminating pregnancies in the case of incest or rape.[24] Sacred anthropologists affirm women by showing compassion, listening to them, standing with them, and rejecting any laws that deny them agency or rob them of freedoms given to them by their Creator. In this way, the sacred anthropologist enthusiastically joins the witness of Jesus as one whose advocacy and actions elevate women above the reaches of the powers of paternalism and politicization. Imagining and moving toward a world where sexism and gender bias, like racism, meet the power of the cross of Christ and die embarrassing and complete deaths is the goal of the sacred anthropologist, for the glory of God.

Sacred anthropologists seek to disrupt the progression of social injustice from the normal rhythms of life. The Bible is the authority on Christianity's teachings concerning equality, and the ethics of Jesus Christ serve as the model the church must adopt to become an advocate for equality. However, exposing inequity can be challenging, and finding the sources, culprits, and causes of inequality can prove even more daunting.

The work of sacred anthropology involves at least a basic understanding of laws and the function and inner workings of government, public policy, history, culture, public health systems, the criminal justice system, and theology, just to name a few of the interdisciplinary subjects that affect image bearers daily. For instance, in his noteworthy tome *The Color of Law*, Richard Rothstein exposes and traces the US government's complicity in housing discrimination. Such knowledge is important to have as the church endeavors to do ministry in urban contexts where there are high rates of crime, drugs, and poverty. When the church attempts to tackle the malaise of problems in these communities, a personal responsibility approach, or a pull yourself up by your own bootstrap mentality, prevails. These approaches, which usually stem from a failure of the church and its ministers to understand the depths and history of these issues, generate frustration and mistrust between the church and the community. Rothstein states,

> Racial segregation in housing was not merely a project of southerners in the former slaveholding Confederacy. It was a nationwide project of the federal government in the twentieth century, designed and implemented by its most liberal leaders. Our system of official segregation was not the result of a single law that consigned African Americans to designated neighborhoods. Rather, scores of racially explicit laws, regulations, and government practices combined to create a nationwide system of urban ghettos, surrounded by white suburbs. Private discrimination also played a role, but it would have been considerably less effective had it not been embraced and reinforced by government.[25]

One racial inequity creates a myriad of other social crises with cascading ramifications. They are almost always interrelated. Economic investments in impoverished communities on any level are minuscule. Where there is poverty, there is crime. When ghettos are created and sustained, crime, overpolicing, and mass incarceration ensue. Alexander Natapoff comments on how America's misdemeanor system cripples individuals and adds to communal and family dysfunction:

> Approximately 13 million people are charged with crimes as minor as littering or as serious as domestic violence. Those 13 million misdemeanors make up the vast majority, around 80 percent, of the nation's criminal dockets. Most arrests in this country are for misdemeanors. Most convictions are misdemeanors. Most Americans will experience the criminal system at the misdemeanor level. Through this enormous process, millions of people are arrested, charged, booked, perhaps jailed, convicted, and punished in ways that can haunt them and their families for the rest of their lives. While mass incarceration has

become recognized as a multi-billion-dollar dehumanizing debacle, it turns out that the misdemeanor behemoth does quieter damage on an even grander scale.[26]

When one considers the numerous police shootings and killings that have stemmed from simple traffic stops, sales of loose cigarettes, and other misdemeanors, the social impact on image bearers is devastating.[27] Bryan Stevenson's work at the Equal Justice Initiative (EJI) has shed light on the massive levels of injustice in America's criminal justice system, some of which affect children. Stevenson and EJI report that over 4,500 juveniles are housed in adult facilities on any given day and that all states have the capacity to house them separately, but many choose not to. As a result, children housed in adult facilities are nine times more likely to commit suicide than those who are housed in juvenile facilities.[28] Michelle Alexander's *The New Jim Crow* and Reuben Johnathan Miller's *Halfway Home: Race, Punishment, and the Afterlife of Mass Incarceration* not only challenge our myth of "paying one's debt to society" for formerly incarcerated individuals but also reveal the glaring disparities, along racial lines, that exist in our criminal justice system.[29] Sacred anthropology is a biblical examination of these life-and-death cultural issues.

Third, cultural anthropology is imperative in helping preachers understand the people who hear their sermons. In this way, as we will see later in chapter 3, sacred anthropology dispels myths that are often propagated by those outside the culture. Social crisis preaching is a critical component of sacred anthropology. The most effective preachers immerse themselves in reading beyond their interests, cultural location, and social interactions. Since many social crises occur between warring factions, any responsible and effective attempt to leverage the gospel on these issues would require the preacher to be aware of the customs, beliefs, values, and fears of the people involved. Too often, preachers irresponsibly (and sometimes hurtfully) hurl suggestions at communal problems for which they have no understanding, experience, and learning. Those who engage from these privileged positions often lack compassion and any understanding beyond the experiences of their communities. One of the chief responsibilities of any preacher is to understand those who hear our sermons. Culturally intelligent preachers possess the skills required to help diverse congregations navigate complex social issues.

Matthew D. Kim, in his groundbreaking book *Preaching with Cultural Intelligence: Understanding the People Who Hear Our Sermons*, has effectively argued that cultural intelligence is needed among congregations and most importantly preachers. Kim argues correctly when he contends that "the preacher who displays cultural intelligence when preaching is simultaneously and subconsciously building bridges between and among his congregants, who often come from very dissimilar cultural contexts. Congregational intelligence is a trait that is sorely missing in many churches today."[30]

Sacred Anthropology: Prophetic Radicalism for Pulpit and Pew introduces a pastoral and congregational theology with both theological and practical insights. This book is designed to prepare and equip the church with a will and a means to "do the truth" by disturbing and disrupting the contemporary crises that rob humanity of the ability to reach its full potential in Christ and God's world.

2

Prophetic Radicalism
Jesus as Priest, Prophet, and King

PROPHETIC RADICALISM HAPPENS when Christians engage in Christian proclamation and living that *expose* the root causes of injustice while *advocating* for God's redemptive justice and simultaneously *acting* as agents of disruption in accord with the life and ministry of Christ through the power of the Holy Spirit. Prophetic radicalism disturbs and disrupts the normality of evil in the world by offering Christ-exalting theologies, worldviews, practices, and proclamations of liberation as alternative forms of living. Since injustice is often embedded in the ideologies and structures of dominant culture and religion, the pastor and pew act as disciples of disruption and disturbance wherever injustice seeks to parade as acceptable values within our culture.

Through his life and his proclamation of the kingdom of God, Jesus Christ embodied a radical resistance to the exclusive and oppressive ideologies and practices that existed in the social and sacred spheres of his day. However, some evangelicals object to viewing and proclaiming the life of Christ as a model for upsetting unjust power structures and combatting the *isms* in our society. Prophetic radicalism is rooted in who Christ is, what he did, and what he is doing. The life and proclamation of Jesus Christ serve as a template for the church to radically confront and ultimately transform the exclusive and oppressive ideologies and practices of our day. Thus, Jesus Christ serves as a model that beckons the pulpit and pew to a life of proclamation and living that *exposes* the root causes of injustice and *advocates* for God's redemptive justice while *acting* in accord with the life and ministry of Christ through the power of the Holy Spirit.

Prophetic radicalism has often been demonstrated through the historic prophetic witness of the Black church. Born out of rejection and resistance, the Black church, from its embryonic existence as the invisible institution in hush harbors, has followed the template of Christian resistance to confront the societal exclusion and oppression that its members face. Historically, the prophetic Black church has been the conscience of our nation on all issues pertaining to marginalized Black and brown communities. In this current era of Christian nationalism and the continuing shadow of Trumpist politics, when false cultural nostalgia threatens to "take back" hard-fought rights and freedoms, prophetic radicalism is the most viable means of modeling Christ in the world.

While this book, at times, makes no apologies for lauding the faithful witness of the Black church, it does not seek to elevate, make exclusive, or monopolize the Black church's claim to prophetic witness. One need only look to the examples of William Lloyd Garrison, Francis Asbury, John Brown, Susan B. Anthony, Dorothy Day, Walter Rauschenbusch, Barbara Brown Taylor, Walter Brueggemann, Miguel A. De La Torre, Leah Schade, Sally A. Brown, and countless others to see that prophetic witness is open to followers of many Christian traditions. As Dan McKanan explains, the American radical tradition has always been collaborative: "It is the tradition of abolitionists who called on their neighbor to immediately renounce the sin of slavery, of feminists who recognized patriarchy as itself a form of slavery, of socialists who labored to build a 'cooperative common-wealth,' and of pacifists who saw war as the ultimate affront to humanity."[1]

However, in the United States, the Black church's profound impact on the social, political, and economic landscape has been unmatched by any other cultural expression of Christianity or secular institution. For that reason, this book draws primarily from the interpretive, homiletical, and activist examples set forth by the Black church.

Prophetic Radicalism: The Work of Christ

Throughout the New Testament, the ministry of Jesus is one of salvation, exposing evil and injustice, advocating for the marginalized and oppressed, and acting in the power of the Holy Spirit to liberate the spiritually and socially oppressed. Jesus is a liberator; to see or read Him as anything else is a misinterpretation of why and to whom he was sent (Luke 4:18). His liberating activity is radical; it strikes at the root. Jesus performs prophetic radicalism in his theocratic role as priest, prophet, and king. I believe that Jesus's saving work in these three offices is not limited to spiritual salvation. Rather, the saving work of Christ is one where spiritual rebirth gives way to imagining new social realities, not maintaining old ones (2 Cor 5:16–18; Eph 2:11–14). These two should be inseparable and indissoluble. Furthermore, I argue that these offices expand beyond personal piety, making them relevant for the church to employ against racial and social oppression. This is a matter of utmost importance because prophetic radicalism provides a lens to critique how the church interprets and sees Jesus and how it weighs the priorities and ramifications of his earthly ministry. Believers who see Jesus Christ as the fulfillment of priest, prophet, and king cannot limit these redemptive functions to only spiritual meanings. Jesus's roles as priest, prophet, and king were played out in the social, political, and economic order. It is vitally important that the church adopts and includes the social impact of Jesus's theocratic offices.

The theocratic offices (priest, prophet, king) of Jesus Christ are the vision and work of God exemplified. John Calvin introduced the theocratic offices of Christ with the argument that the Father bestowed the three offices upon Christ to mediate his work to his creation. The saving activity of Christ, according to Calvin, is threefold and so expressed in these three terms "in order that faith may find a firm basis for salvation in Christ, and thus rest in him." For Calvin, the three offices are biblical terms that most clearly and soundly articulate, through doctrine, what God has done in Christ. Concerning the prophetic office, Calvin states, "God, by providing his people with an unbroken line of prophets, never left them without useful doctrine sufficient for salvation."[2] From a chronological standpoint, Jesus as prophet speaks the word of God as the *Word* of God. As the "high priest," he "is seated at the right hand of the throne of the Majesty in heaven" (Heb 8:1). Jesus makes the once and for all sacrifice, atoning for our individual and corporate sins as well as our spiritual and social sins. He is the risen king who reigns over death, hell, and the grave and all abuses and misuses of earthly power.

As for the theocratic offices, Jesus accomplishes this divine mystery "without dissolving the three unique ministries into one or dismantling their individuality," explains Robert Smith Jr. "Christ simply balanced and embodied all three offices into his personhood."[3] Jesus fulfills the offices of priest, prophet, and king. The Heidelberg Confession declares Jesus "our chief Prophet and Teacher, who has fully revealed to us the secret counsel and will of God concerning our redemption."[4] Helmut Thielicke extends Calvin's argument about the theocratic office of Christ by stating, "When Christ is called prophet, priest, and king, Old Testament themes are both adopted and yet at the same time transcended."[5] By extending Calvin's argument, Thielicke argues that Jesus not only proclaims the will of God but is the embodiment of God's will.

The person and work of Jesus Christ in these three offices is a portrait of prophetic radicalism. Jesus consistently exposes evil and injustice in the religious and secular systems of his day. He is an advocate for women and disadvantaged persons, and the Bible always portrays him, as James Cone suggests, "on the side of the oppressed."[6] Most importantly, through the prophetic radicalism exemplified in Jesus's ministry, he acts as a disrupter of the rhythms of injustice through his preaching and life example.

The message of the kingdom of God, as it was proclaimed by Jesus Christ and the work that God accomplished through Christ on the cross, is nothing short of radical. Jesus is the ultimate prophet. He is the Great High Priest. He is the King of kings. Continuing his ministry in the spirit and nature of the Old Testament prophets, the earthly ministry of Jesus marks him as the obedient, heaven-sent Son of God; chief herald of the kingdom of God; preeminent enemy of Satan, sin, and evil; and exemplar of God's vision for humanity. Jesus called his disciples to embody this same prophetic radicalism: "Proclaim as you go, saying, 'The kingdom of heaven is at hand.' Heal the sick, raise the dead, cleanse lepers, cast out demons" (Matt 10:7–8). Both pastor and pew engage in prophetic radicalism as followers of Christ while modeling Jesus's ministry. There is no realm to which the Spirit of Christ does not have access. Jesus invaded the realms of the political, economic, social, and religious order with proclamations of the kingdom of God. "He who is the blessed and only Sovereign, the King of kings and Lord of lords" (1 Tim 6:15) exemplifies prophetic radicalism in his being and proclamation by *exposing* the root causes of injustice and *advocating* for redemptive justice through his powerful *action*.

Christ and the Theocratic Offices

The work of Christ is multifaceted. The doctrine of the threefold office was developed to describe the varied aspects of Christ's ministry. It holds that Jesus fulfils three theocratic roles—priest, prophet, and king—all of which are necessary for the salvation of God's people. The application of prophetic radicalism can be glimpsed in the theocratic offices by recognizing that, like Jesus, we must actively confront the various manifestations of sin in different ways. It is not uncommon to find the theocratic offices in evangelical theology, but their practical application often falls short and focuses solely on the spiritual aspects of salvation, while the social ramifications of our fallen world are often unaddressed in their teaching and preaching. Seeing Christ in the theocratic offices provides a fresh and unique lens to interpret Jesus's work and by which the church can apply the concept of prophetic radicalism, which is to love neighbor and to engage in Christlikeness.

In his office as High Priest, Jesus both makes the sacrificial offering and becomes the sacrificial offering. As Prophet, he proclaims the word of God to individuals and the nations who trample the righteousness of God. Christ "is the blessed and only Sovereign, the King of kings and Lord of lords" (1 Tim 6:15), who will reign in eternity after having put all enemies under his feet. The Heidelberg Confession declares Jesus "our chief Prophet and Teacher, who has fully revealed to us the secret counsel and will of God concerning our redemption."[7] God's will for spiritual redemption in Christ is also inseparable from the social impact of Jesus's fulfilment as priest, prophet, and king.

JESUS AS PRIEST: HOLINESS AND PROPHETIC RADICALISM

Prophetic radicalism is a holy undertaking. Biblical holiness is vertical and horizontal. Holiness is an inner reality made possible through the finished work of Christ, whereby the fruit of holiness is seen in the ethical conduct and behaviors revealed in our human relationships. Both Old Testament and New Testament articulations of what it means to be holy put social application at the center. In Leviticus, holiness is about both the presentation of one's sacrifice before a Holy God *and* how we sacrifice for our neighbor (Lev 19:5, 9–10). In the New Testament, the embodiment of holiness is made clear by Peter's exhortation: "Having purified your souls by your obedience to the truth for a sincere brotherly love, love one another earnestly from a pure heart" (1 Pet 1:22). Holiness is seen in both pure hearts and clean hands. Holiness is concerned with spiritual convictions and social conduct (1 Pet 2:11–12). We must challenge contemporary readers of the Bible to reconsider the meaning of holiness to include ethical and moral behaviors in the communities where their neighbors work, worship, and play. When holiness is confined to ritualistic individualism or corporate exclusivism, gifts and rules serve to undermine neighborly love and service to the community.

When I was a boy, my friends and I were often perplexed at the Christians who attended the "sanctified church." These fine people defined Christianity through the lens of holiness, but their concept of holiness was defined by emotional (or spiritual) feeling, strict dress codes, and prohibitions on playing cards, going to movies, and dancing. For them, holiness was also expressed in one's ability to exercise any number of spiritual gifts, while they viewed those who did not practice those spiritual gifts as inferior Christians and thus unholy. For me and my friends, on the other hand, the word *holiness* was foreign and unspoken in our Christian circles; it was not part of our ecclesiastical vocabulary. We did not discuss holiness and its relationship to ethical living. For us, holiness was not a lifestyle of joy that flowed from the realities of being freed from the grasp of sin. Neither did we associate holiness with the responsibility to advocate for justice in our community. As I grew older, I realized that I, my friends, and those who attended the sanctified church had a very limited perception of what it really meant to be holy.

For example, we held the unspoken belief that holiness is a spiritual experience and existential reality separate from our secular and social involvement. This concept of holiness is unbiblical and thus unholy. Jesus is our example. He is one without sin, perfect in holiness, the express image of the one Holy God, *and* an advocate for the downtrodden and disinherited. Christlike holiness is not limited to worship inside the walls of the church, where the display of spiritual gifts (laying on of hands, speaking in tongues, prophecy, worship in song, etc.) is only activated on Sunday mornings. Christlike holiness extends beyond the boundaries of brick and mortar to the fringes of society, where the poor experience soul- and body-crushing ordeals daily. Holiness is a lifestyle mostly realized in our actions towards other people.

To understand the priestly office, it is helpful to understand the historical duties of the temple priests, which are outlined in the books of Hebrews and Chronicles.[8] The temple priests of Jesus's day played an important community role and were looked upon as a standard of holiness. In addition to teaching Torah, they also offered prayer and made atonement for sins by standing as intermediaries between Israel's Holy God and God's often-wayward people. Unlike these other priests, Christ had no need to offer sacrifices daily because he did this once and for all when he offered up himself. Jesus fulfills the office of priest through both his work and his existence as the Holy One.

In his office as priest, Jesus embodies the Holiness Code set forth in Leviticus 17–26. Robin C. McCall states, "The Holiness Code makes clear by the nature of its laws that holiness is realized in active terms, through one's ethics and behavior. . . . The establishment of a community-wide ethic based on the unique worldview of the Holiness School—is the Holiness Code's central concern."[9] Jesus is the Holy Child, Yahweh's Holy Servant "who had no sin," "the Holy One of God," and the "Holy and Righteous One." Holiness is an attribute of the Triune God and expresses God's perfection, beauty, and glory. In the Old Testament, holiness is also an attitude lived out in ritual and communal relationship for the people who are created in God's image. As a covenant people, Israel is commanded "to be holy to me, for I the Lord am holy and have separated you from the peoples, that you should be mine."[10]

The New Testament offers a model of holiness in Jesus Christ. Kent Brower explains, "Jesus is re-creating the holy people, centered on him, 'the Holy One of God' (Mark 1:24; John 6:69). This reshaped remnant is doing the will of God, pressing back to the foundations of loving God with one's whole heart and the neighbor as oneself."[11] Jesus demonstrates holiness in his priestly office by obliterating the boundaries that the unholy were once forbidden to cross in the temple. He *is* the temple that, if destroyed, would be raised up in three days (John 2:19). He restores and does not exclude (Matt 8:1–4); he makes clean and does not ostracize (Luke 8:43–48); he makes whole and does not disenfranchise (Mark 5:1–19). Jesus embodies holiness by acting not only in the office of priest but also as the Second Person of the Triune God, whose nature is holiness. Holiness is the mark of people who serve a holy God by following Christ's example; in the case of the priestly office, this includes advocacy for the poor and outcasts. For Jesus, holiness is not limited to the temple, nor is it solely a matter of personal salvation.

The New Testament witness sets forth a standard and prescription for Christian living through the stories of Christ's works, but it also models a way that we might lead holy lives together within a congregational setting. In the New Testament, Christians of the diaspora were to maintain the standard of holiness throughout Asia Minor, despite the existential threat of Roman imperialism and domination. Maintaining the standard of holiness was not the maintenance of rules or something that is earned; rather, it was based on the realization of what Christ has done for us. This model of holiness was *intentional* for Christians, who were "called to live cruciform lives, shaped by the cross and resurrection of Christ, empowered by the Spirit to act in God's mission and reflecting his being before the world,"[12] even when they were oppressed and forced underground. Holiness therefore was—and *is*—an act of political resistance.

The Holiness Code was delivered to Moses inside the tent of meeting, but it was meant to govern daily interactions and the normal dealings of the community. Prophetic radicalism rescues holiness as a concept and practice that has been held hostage inside the church and returns it to the wider community sphere. Pastors and congregations can restore holiness as a concept and practice to be lived everywhere: in grocery stores, city halls, hospitals, and boardrooms; in small rural towns, inner-city schools, and crime-riddled neighborhoods.

Holiness is often viewed as a private and individual matter, where the goals of Christian living are personal piety and purity and the focus is dedicated almost exclusively to the Third Person of the Trinity, as the One who possesses and fills the believer. This view of holiness is one where "right" living is defined by chastity, purity, abstinence from alcohol, strict and devout ritualism, and the denial of worldly pleasures. Defined this way, holiness is highly individualistic and encourages believers to disengage and separate themselves from the world rather than exemplifying Christ to the world and serving those whom Christ served.

American Christianity has often embraced this interpretation of holiness, which is often promoted as a personal and individual pursuit and where the individual is encouraged to spend "private" time with their "personal" savior. Donald W. McCullough cautions against the danger of such an individualistic faith: "Those who have been suckled at the breast of American culture will not easily be weaned from the milk of individualism."[13] Although holiness doubtlessly involves some personal aspects, it is not solely a private matter. The Holiness Code is abundantly communal in every aspect. It is meant to be relational and communal.

The true potency of holiness lies not in individuals' abstinence from the unclean and unholy but in how their actions reverberate within their community. Thus, holiness is not about how one *lives outside* and in isolation from community but about how one *lives out* holiness within the community. Nowhere is this mandate more apparent than in Leviticus 19:9–10: "When you reap the harvest of your land, you shall not reap your field right up to its edge, neither shall you gather the gleanings after your harvest. And you shall not strip your vineyard bare, neither shall you gather the fallen grapes of your vineyard. You shall leave them for the poor and for the sojourner: I am the Lord your God." Personal piety that does not have an impact on the community is not a biblical concept.

The Holiness Code encouraged acts of resistance against the dominant culture of the ancient world. For example, it commands that "you shall not do as they do in the land of Egypt, where you lived, and you shall not do as they do in the land of Canaan, to which I am bringing you. You shall not walk in their statutes" (Lev 18:3). These were radical commands from a Holy God to a holy people.

The Holiness Code distinguished Israel as a unique nation with ethics distinct from the nations around it. McCall argues that "to separate the injunctions of the Holiness Code from, first, the culture and circumstances that birthed them and second, the unique theological worldview that under-girds them is to strip them of their meaning and purpose."[14] In our modern context, holiness is a tenet that is emphasized heavily in several Pentecostal and charismatic denominations and believed to transcend racial categories, empower the church to confront social injustice with spiritual power, and foster unity among God's people.[15] Often expressed as a life of sanctification, in Holiness and Pentecostal denominations, holiness is expressed through living a life separated from "the world." Estrelda Y. Alexander observes that "Black Holiness and Pentecostal bodies primarily share similarities in piety, language and starting points that revolve around three related expectations—sanctification, divine healing and a life of personal piety."[16] Holiness is not only how one lives as a person but also how one lives *with* a people. Thus, "You shall not steal; you shall not deal falsely; you shall not lie to one another. You shall not swear by my name falsely, and so profane the name of your God: I am the Lord. You shall not oppress your neighbor or rob him. The wages of a hired worker shall not remain with you all night until the morning" (Lev 19:11–13), erases any dichotomy between private and public expressions of holiness.

Christians who live as social agents carry this call to pursue holiness (Heb 12:14) into the public. However, holiness is not a command from city councils, employment policies, school boards, or the United States Constitution. It is a word and concept that does not fit predominant notions of Christianity in America, and it has fallen out of currency in many churches. It is often used as a one-dimensional term associated with practices that are decidedly outside of the mainstream, including charismatic performance, glossolalia, and prophecy (of the foretelling sort) and speaking in tongues. Prophetic radicalism calls on us to reconsider what holiness means. While the transformative power of God is expressed in the gifts of the Spirit, those gifts are for the community. Holiness should govern the lives of Christ's followers and, inasmuch, serve as the standard by which we confront injustice through the life and proclamation of the church. In the Old Testament, the Holiness Code is for priests and laypeople alike. As McCall emphasizes, "The Holiness Code departs from the earlier Priestly material of Leviticus and the rest of the Pentateuch by requiring the aforementioned combination of ethical behavior and distinctness not merely of Israel's priests, but of all the people of Israel."[17]

Likewise, as a kingdom of priests, we are reminded that "as he who called you is holy, you also be holy in all your conduct, since it is written, 'You shall be holy, for I am holy'" (1 Pet 1:15–16). In fulfilling the theocratic office of priesthood, we must remember Christ's model of holiness. As we reflect upon Christ in this office, we observe how Christians are to live and treat their neighbors through holiness. Prophetic radicalism restores holiness to the community by proclaiming, "Strive for peace with everyone, and for the holiness without which no one will see the Lord" (Heb 12:14). Christ has made us holy.

Because prophetic radicalism is Christian proclamation and living that expose the root causes of injustice and advocate for God's redemptive justice while acting in accord with the life and ministry of Christ through the power of the Holy Spirit, it is holy work. In similar fashion to the work

of the temple performed by the priesthood, the holy work of prophetic radicalism is carried out by members of the church, all of whom are "a royal
priesthood, a holy nation, a people for his own possession" (1 Pet 2:9). The
church carries out the holy work of prophetic radicalism through Christian
proclamation and living as acts of worship, where the local congregation "in
word or deed, do everything in the name of the Lord Jesus, giving thanks
to God the Father through him" (Col 3:17).

JESUS AS PROPHET

Jesus is the fulfillment of Yahweh's promise to "raise up a prophet like
you from among [our] brothers" so that he will speak for God and do
as God commands (Deut 18:18). In the New Testament, the writer of
Hebrews echoes this promise by declaring, "God spoke to our fathers by the
prophets, but in these last days he has spoken to us by his Son" (Heb 1:1–2).
Jesus fulfills the theocratic office as prophet by continuing in the Old Testament's model as One commissioned by God to speak God's word. However,
Jesus not only speaks the word but also is the Word, as John describes him:
"the Word became flesh and dwelt among us, and we have seen his glory,
glory as of the only Son from the Father, full of grace and truth" (John
1:14). There are three ways by which Jesus continues this tradition: as a
spokesperson for God; as one who, like the prophet Jeremiah, shares God's
burden for the community; and as One who sees and communicates the
vision of God for humanity.

Jesus as Prophet Who Speaks for God

Prophetic radicalism acknowledges Jesus as Savior and prophet. Jesus
is the prophet par excellence, who sees and identifies the evil intentions
in the hearts of humanity and calls for the destruction of the systems and
structures where those evil intentions are carried out. Both pulpit and pew
must proclaim this Christ in all his prophetic glory. Jesus was the ultimate
prophet, "the prophet anticipated from the time of Moses, the prophet
par excellence by whom all other prophets were measured."[18] God spoke
to Moses, concerning Israel, to "raise up for them a prophet like you from

among their brothers. And I will put my words in his mouth, and he shall speak to them all that I command him" (Deut 18:18). Jesus is the fulfillment of that promise. In John 5:46, Jesus affirms this pronouncement with a self-identifying declaration: "He wrote of me." Moses was a radical prophet, confronting the Egyptian monarchy with the liberating word of God. Moses was a deliverer, a liberator, and friend of God. Moses brought deliverance to Israel spiritually by receiving the commandments (Exod 20) and socially, politically, and economically by traversing the Red Sea en route to the land promised to them (Exod 13:7–40:38). Jesus was a prophet like Moses. In word and deed, Jesus continued the tradition of the prophets of Israel as bold representatives who precisely proclaimed the kingdom and justice of God. To proclaim Christ is to proclaim his prophetic identity as a spiritual and social liberator. Any proclamation that excludes one or the other is incomplete. Prophetic radicalism is *Christian proclamation and living that expose the root causes of injustice and advocate for God's redemptive justice while acting in accord with the life and ministry of Christ through the power of the Holy Spirit.*

Ro'eh, or "seer," is among the terms used to describe the prophet and his role in the Old Testament (1 Sam 9:9, 11; 2 Kgs 17:13; *ro'eh*). However, the word more commonly associated with the prophet is *nābî*, which Harris, Archer, and Watke describe as "someone who speaks on behalf of and interprets the will of a supernatural being; often rebuking or predicting events."[19] The prophet is one who speaks for Yahweh and communicates Yahweh's vision and will to the people to whom they are sent. The biblical record gives evidence of Yahweh's words "coming to" the prophet or the prophet being filled with Yahweh's word.[20] Yahweh imparts Yahweh's word through Moses, who asks in the voice of God, "Who has made man's mouth? Who makes him mute, or deaf, or seeing, or blind? Is it not I, the Lord? Now therefore go, and I will be with your mouth and teach you what you shall speak" (Exod 4:11–12). As a spokesperson, a prophet promotes the agenda of God through the power of the Holy Spirit.

The prophet's utterances were sometimes concerned with future events through the predictive element of *foretelling* (Isa 8; 20:1–6; Jer 30:1–9; Amos 9:11–15; Mal 4:2). Likewise, prophetic utterances were also *forthtelling*, *speaking directly to nations and political powers concerning events taking place in their time.* In some cases, we see the same prophet engaged in both performances (foretelling and forthtelling) simultaneously when speaking to the nation, as with Jeremiah's encouragement for the exilic community to "seek the welfare of the city" and then exhorting, "I will fulfill to you my promise and bring you back to this place" (Jer 29:7, 10).

In addition to speaking to or against nations, forthtelling addresses political and religious authorities and, at times, the prophet's own people (Exod 3:10; 4:22–23; 7:16; 2 Kgs 22:7–14; Ezek 13:1–10; Jer 29:1–9; Zech 1:1–6; Mal 1:2–14). It is no secret that the same prophet could engage in both foretelling and forthtelling. These messages to the nations and Israel were often in a continuous loop, one after the other, each intertwined with the other to communicate a full vision of Yahweh's message. Jesus's message to the cities who failed to see and interpret his mighty works is a demonstration of this forthtelling and foretelling dynamic. His rebuke, "Woe to you, Bethsaida! For if the mighty works done in you had been done in Tyre and Sidon, they would have repented long ago in sackcloth and ashes. But I tell you, it will be more bearable on the day of judgment for Tyre and Sidon than for you" (Matt 11:21–22) contains a present warning and a prediction of future consequences. Like the prophets, Jesus denounces evil and pronounces the future consequences of sin and injustice. To embrace Jesus as Savior is to also embrace him as prophet.

Jesus came proclaiming the kingdom of God as a matter of priority: "But seek first the kingdom of God" (Matt 6:33). From his childhood (Luke 2:49) to his crucifixion (Luke 23:42–43), the kingdom of God was important in the life and preaching of Jesus Christ (Luke 2:49), who lived under the domain of a powerful Roman government that brutally crushed dissent (John 19:12–16). He was the prophet sent to speak God's word on behalf of God. He is recognized as the prophet in the gospels by the Samaritan woman (John 4:19). Of Jesus, Timothy Green writes, "His critiques of abusive power and religious exclusivity are reminiscent of prophets such as Amos, Micah, and Isaiah."[21] Jesus's words "Repent, for the kingdom of heaven is at hand" can be viewed as both forthtelling and foretelling

(Matt 4:17). His warning to "repent" is an imperative meant for his listening audience to heed, while his proclamation "for the kingdom of heaven is at hand" is a declaration of the present and coming kingdom of God.

To embrace Jesus as prophet is to preach the kingdom in real time. It is Christian proclamation and living that expose the root causes of injustice while advocating for God's redemptive justice, and simultaneously acting as agents of disruption in accord with the life and ministry of Christ through the power of the Holy Spirit. Social crisis preaching (a component of prophetic radicalism), like prophetic speech, is concerned with both foretelling and forthtelling. Foretelling is the consequential ramification that follows forthtelling. Forthtelling is the warning or admonition that precedes foretelling. In this way, the two are partners that complement each other. As Walter Brueggemann describes, "The themes of prophetic hope are fairly constant. There is nothing here that is private, spiritual, romantic, or otherworldly. It is always social, historical, this-worldly, political, economic. The dream of God and the hope of Israel are for the establishment of a new social order which will embody peace, justice, freedom, equity, and well-being."[22]

Like such prophets as Elijah, Micah, and Amos, Jesus rebukes those who abuse their power and privilege. Reminiscent of Jeremiah, he proclaims hope and redemption amid despair and hopelessness. As a radical prophet, Jesus cries out against sin in any form and preaches an inclusive, ethical community where passions and practices align with God's intention of human flourishing for all. The foretelling function of social crisis preaching anchors the message of God in the future promised and guaranteed in the Old and New Testaments. Foretelling insists that *current spiritual* conditions may have *future social* ramifications. It can be seen in Isaiah's proclamation, "If you are willing and obedient, you shall eat the good of the land; but if you refuse and rebel, you shall be eaten by the sword" (Isa 1:19–20). Prophetic preaching engages the foretelling dimension of prophetic utterances when the preacher boldly proclaims what God has promised about the destiny of the wicked and the oppressor as well as God's coming vindication for the poor and the oppressed. Concerning forthtelling, the preacher proclaims what is right and what is just in the here and now, recalling the wicked and the just alike to the standards of God's righteousness. Pastors and congregations who engage in prophetic radicalism must proclaim God's truths and apply those truths in intentional ways that promote redemption, justice, and peace.

Jesus as Prophet Who Feels

Abraham Heschel raises the question, "What manner of man is the prophet?"[23] This is a question of constitution. It probes the deep and inner being of those whom God calls to represent him. Heschel's question is meant to examine the makeup and composition of those who have heard the *vox deo* (voice of God), seen the vision, and surrendered in vulnerability to the unrelenting tug of Yahweh's demand. Regarding the Old Testament prophets, Heschel states, "The prophet is a man who feels fiercely. God has thrust a burden upon his soul, and he is bowed and stunned at man's fierce greed."[24] Thus, above all, the prophet's constitution is one of sensitivity to the passion of God. Jesus is the prophet who is touched by the feelings of our infirmities (Heb 4:15), and he is moved by the slightest sight of human misery. As the prophet who feels, he weeps (John 11:35), he has compassion for the disinherited and dispossessed (Mark 9:36), and he touches and heals through love (Matt 8:3).

Heschel goes on to write, "To the prophets even a minor injustice assumes cosmic proportions."[25] And from this emotional urgency, the prophet proclaims what God has declared right and good. Unlike the prosperity gospel's interpretation of the prophet as a thermostat, manipulating the emotional temperature of the people, God's prophet acts as a carefully calibrated thermometer to announce God's white-hot outrage against perpetrators of injustice. The prophet is God's spokesperson who feels. Jesus bore the hallmarks of compassion in his prophetic role. Ultimately, his willingness to feel was manifested in the brutality and shame he endured at Calvary. For us he died. Like so many prophets before him, he preached redemption, *and* like no prophet before him, his resurrection sealed our redemption. How might the church that practices prophetic radicalism honor the prophetic office of Christ? We profess him as prophet, and we must, like him, be prophetic.

Jesus as Prophet Who Sees

Jesus embodies the prophetic office through his discernment and obedience to God's will. The prophet Jonah knows God's will, flees from God's will, and then later reluctantly obeys. Jesus, knowing God's will, in resignation cries, "Nevertheless, not my will, but yours, be done" (Luke 22:42). Prophets were called into the will of God through revelation. Knowledge of God's will requires obedience. Jesus is the prophet who, in seeing the will of God, obeys the will of God. His prophetic office was essential to God's redemptive will for humanity.

God grants spiritual insight to the prophets so that they will know God's will and the purposes God has for God's people. The *seer* possesses a pathos of prophetic imagination and envisioning, both of which are enabled by the spirit of the Lord. The *seer*, then, can discern the zeitgeist (the spirit of the times) and has the foresight to capture possibilities of justice and human harmony while possessing the wherewithal to see through the forces that attempt to thwart those possibilities.

Imagining and envisioning God's vision enable the prophet to articulate that vision with picturesque language to the people of God. Like the seer, the prophet's ability to visualize empowers them to speak with vivid imagery and sharp artistry. Old Testament scholar R. B. Y. Scott precisely describes the prophet's unique responsibility. He states, "The grasp of the moral and spiritual realities of a given situation, coupled with the certainty that he [the prophet] must proclaim them in unmistakable terms, marked off a prophet like Micah or Amos."[26]

In the Bible, a number of prophets had visions that included theophanies—visions of the spellbinding glory of God. The prophet's commission following a vision often called for personal sacrifices, renunciations of sin, and pronouncements of judgment upon the mightiest of nations. For instance, Ezekiel is called to be a prophet in a tumultuous time and under extreme national circumstances. The nature of his calling meets the

intensity of the conditions to which he is called. Ezekiel's call is marked by
the voice of God, heavenly visions (1:4–28), and Spirit possession (2:2). His
call is reminiscent of the call stories of many African American preachers,
pastors, and prophets who were called by God during times marked by
extreme social injustice, national sin, and human oppression. And like Ezekiel, many African American religious leaders center their calling around
ecstatic visions accompanied by the voice of God. The visions of Harriet
Tubman—considered to be the "Moses" of the enslaved, fleeing for freedom
on the Underground Railroad—are well documented. Catherine Clinton
states, "Tubman had been visited by powerful visions, waking dreams that
she felt were sending her messages. . . . The images that haunted Tubman
were graphic and terrifying."[27]

Of Nat Turner's visions, Stephen B. Oates writes,

> He claimed that the Holy Spirit has again spoken to him and had
> opened the heavens themselves—as God has done with Ezekiel in the
> days of the Old Testament—and had shown Nat visions in the sky,
> visions so profound that they took a slave's breath away. And in the
> cabins at night, the slaves gathered around the young mystic, a sea of
> black faces looking on in awe, as Nat described what all he had felt and
> seen. . . . From his slave pulpit, Nat recounted his visions in dramatic
> detail, telling his congregation about the warring angels in the sky,
> about the Savior's arms stretched across Southampton's horizon.[28]

Jesus not only sees the kingdom of God but ushers it in through per-
sonal sacrifice and holy proclamation and living. Prophetic radicalism calls
congregations and pastors to "be wise as serpents and innocent as doves"
(Matt 10:16). In the transfiguration narrative found in Matthew 17:1–13,
Peter, James, and John see Jesus among the prophets Moses and Elijah.
This vision is significant because it reveals to his disciples that Jesus is not
simply a prophet worthy of a tabernacle; he is revealed to them as the
Son of God with whom God is well pleased. Jesus commands them not
to speak of this vision until his resurrection. The New Testament is the

proclamation of Jesus as God's risen Son who acts and speaks like the prophet Moses (Deut 18:18). As his followers, we cannot sanitize nor romanticize Jesus as simply a meek and mild Savior who is only concerned with the finalities of earthly existence. He is the prophet who suffered and died because of the proclamation of a message that violently clashed with the themes of the political and religious order of his day. As prophet, he and his message live in us, the prophetically radical church who, like him, must proclaim the kingdom of God and God's justice.

The word *vision* has found common currency among American preachers for several decades. This word, borrowed from and anchored in Habakkuk 2:2, is consistently used as a metaphor to refer to an idea that a pastor believes they received from God as a command to build or develop an impactful ministry. The pastor's "vision" is usually backed and guaranteed by God (thus the well-worn phrase "where there is vision, there is provision"). The promises contained in the vision may result in an extremely successful, large, impactful ministry, with facilities, resources, and people to match. Thousands of pastors, acting in obedience and faithfulness, have followed the voice of God to labor in building ministries of significant communal, spiritual, and social impact. A large and fruitful ministry does not need to be one whose explosive growth relies on a cross-less gospel or that panders to people looking to achieve material prosperity without worrying about corporate concerns or personal responsibility. Churches and ministries that misappropriate the gospel come in all sizes, shapes, denominations, and cultural persuasions. The visions of these churches not only are built off the backs of the most vulnerable but hardly represent the One whose kingdom stands against materialism, racism, and militarism.

While I will not address the validity or sincerity of these churches or their pastors, what I find amazing is that the "vision" some pastors claim as one that comes from God almost never incorporates an ecclesiology that emphasizes the responsibility of congregations to disrupt the evil systems of injustice by exposing corporate sin and advocating for the poor and disenfranchised. This is an ecclesiological vision that may call for pain and suffering. These pastors seldom describe their "visions" as resisting and challenging the corruption, greed, and idolatry of the rich and powerful, since such a vision might lead to pain and suffering. Jesus suffered ridicule and ultimately death for resisting the valueless standards of the empire, just as the prophet Jeremiah suffered ridicule for calling Israel to repentance. In his theocratic office as prophet, Jesus provides a portrait of prophetic radicalism for modern-day followers in pulpit and pew not simply to gaze in awe but to emulate in our proclamation and living.

JESUS CHRIST AS KING

Prophetic radicalism affirms Jesus as the risen King who, in his resurrection, defeated the imperial powers of Rome, crushed the diabolical political machinery manifested in the cross, took the sting out of death, and robbed the grave of victory. For believers who occupy pulpit and pew and who daily stare down the forces of systemic injustice, hope abounds in Jesus's identity as risen King. Ultimately, the evils of social injustice are eternally defeated. Christ is risen as King. Every act of resistance to the sinful structures that tend to rob humanity of the basic necessities of life should be anchored in the hope that because Jesus reigns over death as King, "we are more than conquerors" (Rom 8:37).

Christ is the expectation of the Messianic kingship. He is the fulfillment of the Davidic covenant in which God promised David to "raise up your offspring after you, who shall come from your body, and I will establish his kingdom. He shall build a house for my name, and I will establish the throne of his kingdom forever" (2 Sam 7:12–13). These words are a part of the Davidic covenant.

Despite the destruction of the temple, exile, and Israel's repetitive slides into idolatry, God fulfills the Davidic promise in Christ. The New Testament witness to God's promise is heralded in angelic proclamation: "And behold, you will conceive in your womb and bear a son, and you shall call his name Jesus. He will be great and will be called the Son of the Most High. And the Lord God will give to him the throne of his father David, and he will reign over the house of Jacob forever, and of his kingdom there will be no end" (Luke 1:31–33). Nathanael recognizes Jesus as king (John 1:49).

Eugene H. Merrill contends, "From the beginning it was the purpose of God to channel his sovereignty over his own people (and, indeed, over all the earth) through a line of kings that would eventuate in the divine Son of God himself."[29] Through the inspiration of the Holy Spirit, this promise was confirmed; as the psalmist testifies, "Once for all I have sworn by my holiness; I will not lie to David. His offspring shall endure forever, his throne as long as the sun before me. Like the moon it shall be established forever, a faithful witness in the skies" (Ps 89:35–37). Nine hundred years after it was given, God fulfilled his covenant through an heir of David's flesh, Jesus of Nazareth.

Various Christian interpretive arguments abound as to how God would fulfill the Davidic covenant. Does this covenant require a literal fulfillment? Is the millennial reign of Christ—for those who subscribe to that specific eschatological doctrine—God's fulfillment of the promise to David? If so, what do we make of the current state of political affairs? The arguments surrounding the fulfillment of the Davidic covenant are beyond the scope of this book. However, I propose that the interpretive lens through which the church views the Davidic covenant is in keeping with how the church interprets the Abrahamic covenant (Gen 12:1–3). The Abrahamic covenant is one of ethical inclusion, not exclusion based on nationality. Jesus fulfills the theocratic office of King in his historical birth and continues the promise through the ushering in of a new kingdom at his birth, established and solidified in his resurrection, where "God placed all things under his feet and appointed him to be head over everything for the church" (Eph 1:22). In this reality, a higher principle and law is established, one in which exclusionary, racist ideologies and cultural supremacy are abolished, making way for peace and reconciliation, since "he has broken down in his flesh the dividing wall of hostility" (Eph 2:14). Prophetic radicalism is embraced as a principle and practiced through ministry and discipleship with enthusiasm through the uncompromising truth given to us by the resurrected King of kings.

In ancient Israel, God's rule was to be carried out through the legislative, judiciary, social, religious, and economic rule of the king. Jesus as Lord and Christ is a political affirmation that lays intentional claims of the superiority of God's rule in Christ. The angel's proclamation in Luke 1 comes amid a political climate dominated by authorities who did not tolerate rivals. However, Jesus makes clear that the kingdom he represents is superior in value (Matt 13:44), strength (John 18:36), and justice (Matt 5:38—6:4) and is therefore greater than any earthly kingdom. When he stands before Pilate and Herod, he affirms that he is a king who won't be persuaded, intimidated, or threatened into a subservient role inferior to that ordained of him by God (Matt 26:11–14). This was not the first time he rejected the earthly wishes and cries from crowds to make him a king. After feeding the five thousand, those who witnessed the sign wanted to make him king (John 6:15). But Jesus's self-identifying declaration as "bread of life," who came down from heaven (John 6:35, 41, 50), where no earthly king has ever ruled, represents God's assigned role for him on earth. As risen king, he spoke of his kingdom (Acts 1:3) and gave his disciples (and us) the assurance of power to become witnesses of his kingdom (Acts 1:8). Prophetic radicalism is *Christian proclamation and living that expose the root causes of injustice and advocate for God's redemptive justice while acting in accord with the life and ministry of Christ through the power of the Holy Spirit.*

The theocratic office of Christ as king relates to prophetic radicalism by modeling and teaching a faith that endures the encroachments of empire upon person and community. How is the church able to practice prophetic radicalism? Through the power given to it as a result of Jesus's resurrection and reign over death and the grave. Jesus is the risen king with "all authority in heaven and on earth" (Matt 28:18), who gives the church power to make disciples who will observe all that he commanded (Matt 28:19–20). When Christ is seen as king, salvation takes on a liberative element that is inextricably bound to the spiritual. He is not like an earthly king who may be driven by political loyalties, economic interests, and even personal ambitions that result in the oppression of others rather than their liberation. What does it mean to say that "Jesus is a deliverer" or that "Jesus will set you free"? In the theocratic office as king, Jesus, through his authority and witnesses, has established and is establishing a world where justice, freedom, and equality of citizenship are the orders of the day.

James Harris recognizes that "freedom and equality under God are not abstract philosophical constructs as rationalism, empiricism, or Platonic idealism are. Justice, freedom, and equality are embedded in Christian faith and biblical tradition—something that the strands of evangelicalism seem to ignore."[30] The relevance to Jesus Christ's fulfillment of the theocratic office as King to prophetic radicalism also has everything to do with how God's vision of kingdom serves as the measure of how image bearers are governed in the world. Since children of God live in the world, there should be no realm where God's principles and God's power do not govern. God's word serves as the standard of how we measure fairness, justice, and equity in policies, laws, and procedures. Most importantly, since we embrace Christ as King, we understand that as citizens of earthly kingdoms, our ultimate allegiance is to Christ, who represents the kingdom of God. Therefore, when human laws are unjust, the decrees of God must stand as a testimony against them. As such, prophetic radicalism sermonizes and proclaims Jesus as king and ruler in a world where human power attempts to overwhelm and overshadow the hope that resides in God's kingdom and in Christ.

Our lives are aligned against any notion that lifts America or any other nation above or equal to God's kingdom. Since we embrace Jesus as king, we can critique our earthly kingdoms, levy corrective rebukes, and work to eradicate and dismantle any forms of systemic and structural injustices by means that align with the love ethic and character of God in Christ, who was raised from death to rule over all.

Conclusion: Prophetic Radicalism as Life and Being

Prophetic radicalism is centered in Jesus Christ and articulates a pastoral theology that includes both pastor and congregation. Through the power of the spirit of Christ, the will of God is communicated to the forces of evil, both by proclamation of the word and through activism that is anchored in that proclaimed word. Thus, prophetic radicalism employs the ethics of Christ, which is the fruit of the Spirit to disarm evil, to inform those who are blind to and have bought into the everyday norms that perpetuate injustice, and to practice resistance for the good of the community. By his ultimate triumph over all forces of evil—spiritual, social, economic, and political—his eternal kingship gives the church hope in the affirmation, "the kingdom of the world has become the kingdom of our Lord and of his Messiah, and he will reign for ever and ever" (Rev 11:15).

Prophetic radicalism is rooted in the life and proclamation of Jesus Christ. The theocratic offices provide pastors and congregations a metaphor and image to anchor their theological framework and practical expressions. Prophetic radicalism extends beyond the pulpit to the pew. It is a way of life and living. Prophetic witness for the Lord includes *kerygmatic* boldness. Prophetic witness is a reflection of Christian faithfulness. To be a witness μάρτυς (martyr) is the most radical expression of the Christian faith because it marries life with proclamation, creating a prophetic ethos in the vein of the prophets and Jesus Christ.

Prophetic radicalism stems from the New Testament admonition to be Christ's witnesses (Acts 1:8), but it also keeps harmony with the historical prophetic standard exhibited in the Black church, where preacher and parishioner live lives of prophetic resistance amid a world that defined them as less than human. The Christian prophetic witness derives its radical quality from the fact that people, from the Old Testament to the present age, gave or were willing to give their lives for the cause of justice for all image bearers. While proclamation and living are the essential, intertwined, and inseparable elements for effective prophetic radicalism, where one is dependent on the other for potency, its intra-Trinitarian element is the concept that makes prophetic radicalism distinctly Christian. Throughout the ages, Christian witness at its best has exemplified Spirit-empowered commitment to the values of the kingdom of God on earth through the love ethic and cross-bearing example of Jesus Christ. Therefore, prophetic radicalism is *Christian proclamation and living that expose the root causes of injustice and advocate for God's redemptive justice while acting in accord with the life and ministry of Christ through the power of the Holy Spirit.*

The Sacred Anthropologist

Race, Injustice, and People in the Pews

UNFORTUNATELY, WE FIND ourselves in the twenty-first century still struggling with the issues of race and racism. Police brutality tops the list of tension-filled topics dividing Americans into racial camps. During the second half of the 2010s, many African Americans died at the hands of police officers. In addition to the notable murders of Breonna Taylor, George Floyd, Terence Crutcher, Jordan Edwards, Botham Jean, and Daunte Wright, the murders of dozens of other unarmed African Americans deserve equal national attention and outcry. Nathaniel Picket II was shot by a San Bernardino County, California, sheriff's deputy in 2015. Picket, who suffered from mental illness, was unarmed and less than one hundred feet from his front door at the time of the shooting.[1] Ronell Foster was shot and killed by the police in Vallejo, California, in 2018, after being stopped for riding his bicycle without a light.[2] Tony M. Green Jr. was shot and killed by a Kingsland, Georgia, police officer on June 20, 2018, following a traffic stop.[3]

The recent discussions about the teaching of critical race theory in high schools and universities is another subject that has sparked racial division, clearly splitting individuals and political parties along racial lines, with white Republican governors in several southern states "banning" critical race theory from schools even though most high schools across America have never included the subject in their curriculum.[4] Even discussions about the Covid-19 pandemic have racial connotations, since social determinants indicate that minority communities have less access to quality health care, fewer opportunities for Covid-19 literacy, and less access to vaccination sites and opportunities. The Center for Disease Control states, "Discrimination, which includes racism, shapes social and economic factors that put people at increased risk of severe COVID-19 illness."[5]

Then there is the prominent issue of voting rights. On April 17, 2021, congresswoman Terri Sewell (D-AL-07) introduced the John R. Lewis Voting Rights Advancement Act. This key legislation was meant to restore the vital protections of the historic Voting Rights Act of 1965, which were removed by the Supreme Court in the 2013 *Shelby County v. Holder* decision and the 2021 *Brnovich v. DNC* decision. This bill, referred to as H.R. 4, is aimed to protect voters from racial discrimination and to ensure fair and equal access to the ballot box for Black and minority voters in all elections.[6] Under this bill, as with the Voting Rights Act of 1965, states and munici-palities would be required to apply for clearance from the Department of Justice before revising or changing voting laws. On May 26, 1965, the Voting Rights Act passed the Senate by a vote of 77–19. As recently as 2006, the Voting Rights Act Reauthorization Act, which extended the 1965 Voting Rights Act for twenty-five years, passed the Senate by a vote of 98–0. On January 19, 2022, the John R. Lewis Voting Rights Advancement Act failed to pass in the Senate by a vote of 52–48. Miguel A. De La Torre's precision on this matter is undeniable, as he concludes, "The institutionalized voter suppression—voter purges, felony disenfranchisement, gerrymandering, and voter ID requirements—did not appear ex nihilo: it was and continues to be a strategy by which white supremacy is maintained. The only way white supremacy can remain in power is by short-circuiting democracy with apartheid legislation."[7] As to the question of whether we have made racial progress, one has to wonder if we are slowly sliding into a regressive state. Think of almost any social crisis, and you will find racial connota-tions, racial division, and historic racial turbulence at the root and center.

Who Is the Sacred Anthropologist?

Sacred anthropology is *the conveyance of a concept that applies prophetic radicalism to understanding the social order so that we can affect a biblically based response designed to call the church to a kingdom focus that holistically addresses humanity.* The sacred anthropologist is the person who carries out this concept through prophetic radicalism. Sacred anthropology is inseparable from prophetic radicalism. Recall the definition of prophetic radicalism from chapter 1: *"Prophetic radicalism happens when Christians engage in Christian proclamation and living that expose the root causes of injustice while advocating for God's redemptive justice and simultaneously acting as agents of disruption in accord with the life and ministry of Christ through the power of the Holy Spirit."*

The sacred anthropologist can be a pastor who provides a living example of prophetic radicalism in life and through proclamation. The sacred anthropologist can also be a member of the local body of Christ who serves alongside other members in ministries that call the church to a kingdom focus that holistically addresses humanity. The sacred anthropologist is anyone, whether pulpit or pew, who, through the compassion of Christ and the power of the Holy Spirit, commits to serving and advocating for members of the human family who are often dehumanized and robbed of opportunities because of the sinful attitudes of others and the systems in which those attitudes daily operate.

As stated in chapter 1, sacred anthropology uses an interdisciplinary approach to understand the social order, which includes first and primarily Christian anthropology. The Bible is the catalyst from which the concept of sacred anthropology is cast. It is the primary source and resource from which this concept is argued. Sacred anthropology is committed to what the Bible says about the nature of humanity and humanity's relationship with God and itself. Sacred anthropology is posited as a theological concept committed to the Bible. The sacred anthropologist argues for the truth in the word of God and executes this concept through the power of the Holy Spirit. However, because we recognize that God has gifted people with knowledge and skills outside of the Bible (all truth is God's truth), sacred anthropology also respects and uses the disciplines of cultural anthropology, ethics, hermeneutics, sociology, and ethnography, among others, that shed light on human relationships, culture, and flourishing or the lack thereof. According to the American Anthropological Association, "Anthropology is the study of humans, past and present. To understand the full sweep and complexity of cultures across all of human history, anthropology draws and builds upon knowledge from the social and biological sciences as well as the humanities and physical sciences. A central concern of anthropologists is the application of knowledge to the solution of human problems. Historically, anthropologists in the United States have been trained in one of four areas: sociocultural anthropology, biology/physical anthropology, archeology, and linguistic anthropology."[8]

Every area of anthropology is vital to sacred anthropology. However, since sacred anthropology primarily confronts racial injustice, this concept draws heavily upon the research of experts in sociocultural anthropology.[9] By employing sociocultural anthropology, the sacred anthropologist can use a wealth of research and scientific data to understand the complexities of race, racial structures, and the history of how race and racism have functioned in our churches and society. Christian or theological anthropology is the hermeneutic in which sacred anthropology is launched. Sacred anthropology begins with the presupposition of Genesis 1:27: "God created mankind in his own image, in the image of God he created them; male and female he created them" (NIV).

How Is Sacred Anthropology Done?

A book about sacred anthropology must tackle the problem of race in society and the church head-on.[10] This chapter will provide practical steps on how the pulpit and pew can become sacred anthropologists. This will be my focus for four primary reasons.

First, the sacred anthropologist celebrates ethnicity. This philosophy and practice does not ask anyone to discard ethnicity. It simply encourages

Christians to "love your neighbor as yourself" (Mark 12:31). God created humanity in his image. In God's splendor, glory, majesty, and power, God placed God's imprint on every nationality and ethnicity on earth. To embrace and celebrate our ethnicities *is* a way to celebrate who we are in Christ. I have discovered that African Americans have often been accused of making their culture and ethnicity an idol. We are often asked "not to elevate our ethnicity above our status in Christ." Thus, comments such as "there is no such thing as the Black church, there is but one church" are common expressions of the requirement to discard the beauty of Blackness in order to be accepted and to assimilate the church and "orthodox theology," as defined by white Christians. We seldom ask the question, "Why do we have a Black church?" The Black church was born out of rejection and necessity, the rejection of Black image bearers from white churches. Black Christians also rejected theologies and doctrines that damned Black humans to perpetual slavery. It was necessary for Black Christians to create space for pure and true worship of the Triune God where all God's children would be welcomed and loved. Asking Black Christians to discard "Blackness" is neither necessary nor biblical.

White Christians are not required to use a racial or ethnic modifier to describe their faith, theology, or church. Black Christians and minority cultures were not "at the table" to construct the theologies and churches that denied Black Christians access, expression, and theological input. Thus, by default, evangelical theology is perceived as "white." Christians can embrace the beauty of who they are and be one in Christ with Christians of other ethnicities without having to separate their ethnicity from their salvation. However, when any ethnicity claims superior status and seeks to establish and maintain that status through laws, violence, and structures, the world is not as God intended. The sacred anthropologist respects and appreciates all image bearers regardless of their color, nation of origin, or culture.

Second, as I have already stated, racism is blatant and touches almost every aspect of human life; it is the crisis of the hour. We need tools every Christian can use to confront and fight injustice and racism. It would be negligent to address the social crises of racism without arming the reader with new tools to effectively lead the church out of the dark and long night of racial division and injustice and into the light of a new day to be "the light of the world" (Matt 5:14). To write about racism is to confront it. To act as sacred anthropologists with intentionality and urgency is to make progress where regression is currently looming.

Third, old attempts at racial reconciliation were mostly the expectation of clergy, pastors, and denominational leaders. Pulpit swaps, prayer rallies, and proclamations were and are primarily the sole activity of ordained leaders, with little, if any, involvement from the laity in the pews. Sacred anthropology invites the pulpit and pew into a "priesthood of all believers," "every member in ministry" approach to lead the quest for truth, justice, and reconciliation.

Fourth and lastly, Jesus commands the disciples and the future church to be "the salt of the earth and the light of the world" (Matt 5:13–14). Christians were at the fore of our nation's racial progress during the most contentious racial conflicts—namely, the abolishment of slavery and the eradication of Jim Crow. As I will discuss in chapter 4, the church is armed with the word of God and the spiritual vitality to rise to the occasion once again. I argue that the church has the capacity to heal the racial division in our world.

The sacred anthropologist need not have a degree in anthropology but is required to have a love for humanity and feel a burden to solve the problems that create division and suffering. The sacred anthropologist can glean much from the professional anthropologist in the sacred work of prophetic radicalism. I name four practical and essential means by which sacred anthropology is practiced in a community of believers. The pulpit and pew become sacred anthropologists by

1. being *aware* of our own culture and *appreciating* the culture of others;
2. *analyzing* the available data as well as experiences of socially disadvantaged communities before making moral judgments and enacting crippling policies that fail to help those communities;

3. making *amends* that will affect the masses and that can be measured with tangible and objective markers; and

4. *assisting* other churches and secular agencies in ministry and activities that intentionally disrupt the philosophies, theologies, and practices that tend to normalize racism and injustice.

Appreciating the Other

Anthropologists are professionals who love their work because they have a profound appreciation for other cultures. Although the sacred anthropologist is not required to possess formal training in anthropology, the qualities that enable this concept come from one's desire to listen to and learn from other cultures. The sacred anthropologist is also committed to the Christian ethic to love one's neighbor. We are commanded not just to love one another but to "love the Lord your God with all your heart and with all your soul and with all your mind and with all your strength" and to "love your neighbor as yourself" (Mark 12:30–31). Intrinsic to Christian theology is the love of God and the love of neighbors. The sacred anthropologist appreciates the other by first loving God. Emanating from one's love for God is the love for others. It can also be stated, within the command to love neighbor as ourselves, that we must possess an awareness of ourselves. This begins when we are aware of ourselves as image bearers who have been fearfully and wonderfully made (Ps 139:14). God created each of us with a distinction that flowed from God's profound and powerful position as Creator and Sovereign. One of the ways in which God's beautiful imprint is upon us is through our different ethnic and unique cultural expressions, witnessed primarily in the beauty of language, food, ritual, hairstyle, fashion and dress, history, and music to name a few.

Color blindness fails to acknowledge those expressions. Therefore, "color-blind" Christianity is unbiblical, unnecessary, and unworthy of the Creator's glory because it conceals the grandeur and glory of God. Color-blind theology is the child of a Eurocentric-American dominated reading of Scripture, which, initially with intention and later without effort, cast Jesus as a blond-haired, blue-eyed savior. This image dominated art and portraits of "Jesus," as it was often assumed that Jesus, though being born in Palestine and hidden in Egypt, was indeed white, straight-haired, and keen-nosed and bearing other European features. Colorblind theology contends that Jesus's color doesn't matter. However, Marcus Jerkins powerfully details the flaw and hypocrisy with such claims: "We must be clear: Jesus certainly has a color. The typical response of many that Jesus's color did not matter is fundamentally wrong. It is interesting that many of those people have only been concerned about proclaiming that Jesus had no color, or that his color did not matter, in response to those who say Jesus looked like everyone else in Nazareth of Galilee. They had no problem with Jesus's color while he was imaged as white for centuries. But now there is a problem with Jesus having a color."[11]

Color-blind is blind! Blind to our uniqueness, blind to the complexities of beauty, blind to new outlooks and insights, blind to opportunities, blind to God's creative genius. Color blindness as a Christian aspiration is a misnomer because color blindness represents a cultural worldview and thus a cultural language. The rhetoric of "I don't see race" and "color blindness" is usually defined by and conceived through the cultural understanding of one racial group—those who have the greatest wealth, most powerful positions and influence, and largest numbers. Making this point clear, Jesse Curtis contends that the function of Christian color blindness is "the perpetuation of evangelical whiteness."[12] We are to show forth who we are in our fullest expression in Christ. Hence life in Christ, the One who models human perfection and beauty both within and beyond physical characteristics, permits us to celebrate who God created us to be while we appreciate and celebrate God's creation in other human beings. Jerkins also asserts, "Color-blind theology will not do with a historical reading of the biblical texts . . . we do ourselves a disservice and we misread the biblical narrative if we suggest that skin complexion never mattered in the Bible. It mattered then and it matters now."[13] Christ did not deny or reject his Palestinian identity. Neither did he call the Samaritan woman or the Cyrenian or any other ethnicity to forfeit their identities or persons to be in fellowship with him. Christ does not call us to discard our ethnicities as if we are ghost-like creatures without distinct features, colors, mannerisms, families, or histories. However, Christ does call us to confront the histories, mannerisms, actions, thinking, convictions, and ways in which our ethnicity has positioned us as superior and where our cultural proclivities demean and destroy other image bearers.

The sacred anthropologist shows appreciation for other cultures through an awareness of their own racial presuppositions and the sources from which those presuppositions arise. Unfortunately, we live in a segregated ecclesial and social world. For many of us, life is lived in silos, and few of us can claim a robust multicultural reality in the spaces where we live, work, play, and worship. The sources of our racial stereotypes, prejudices, and presuppositions come from our homogeneous daily lives. Information obtained about other cultures rarely comes from within those cultures but rather from the mounds of misinformation and the misinformed people within our own ranks. Our social and religious networks are comprised of people who look, think, feel, and vote like we do. The sacred anthropologist must push back on disparaging myths about other cultures. Narratives that begin with "I heard that all _____ people are . . ." or "I was always told that . . ." must be rejected and replaced with the truth that comes from living in relationship with one another. Kelly Brown Douglass comments on the blessings of proximity, stating, "Proximity helps transform the collective imagination regarding those who have been socially vilified. It does so by closing the distance between the privileged and those whom the privileged have othered. It brings the othered into the sphere of concern. It helps the privileged to see that those caricatured as not like them are indeed just like them—with bodies that can be hurt and need healing, hearts that can be broken and need love, and souls that can be lost and need salvation."[14]

For the sacred anthropologist, appreciating the other is also exemplified in the desire to know and understand other cultures. Just as professional anthropologists are driven by curiosity, the sacred anthropologist is driven by a sacred curiosity that is influenced by the drive to experience, understand, and love God's presence and participation in the lives of other people. The desire or drive to know is a lesson the sacred anthropologist can learn from the concept of cultural intelligence (CQ). Cultural intelligence is a concept practiced primarily in global business, education, and government sectors that measures the effectiveness of cross-cultural competence and relationships. According to early developers of cultural intelligence Soon Ang and Linn Van Dyne, "Cultural intelligence is the capability to function effectively across national, ethnic, and organizational cultures."[15] Corporate executives view cultural intelligence as an essential and necessary practice for business expansion and success. Cultural intelligence includes four components: CQ drive, CQ knowledge, CQ strategy, and CQ action.[16] The most essential component to the sacred anthropologist, as one who appreciates other cultures, is CQ drive. David Livermore explains, "Leaders with high CQ Drive are motivated to learn and adapt to new and diverse cultural settings."[17] Appreciation is expressed in one's motivation to learn and adapt. Appreciation, like love, "does not insist on its own way" (1 Cor 13:5). The sacred anthropologist models a willingness to live in community with people who are beautifully different.

Cultural intelligence is one's willingness to learn, understand, appreciate, and adapt to different cultures for the sake of mutual good and benefit. In the same way, Christians must acknowledge that in a world growing increasingly more diverse, cultural intelligence is necessary for kingdom growth and ministry effectiveness. The multicultural church must be more than glimpses of token diversity, where diversity is visible in the pews but the leadership, worship styles, and rituals remain white and male dominated.

Analyzing Data and Experiences of Others

As stated above, sacred anthropology takes an interdisciplinary approach, using other disciplines that enable the pulpit and pew to understand and resist the root causes of injustice and to eradicate racism as a daily experience in the life of the church and society. Racism festers, grows, and passes down from one generation to the next through sharing myths, misinformation, and disinformation. As it pertains to human culture and other ethnicities, misinformation exists when there are gaps in information. Disinformation occurs when people deliberately spread myths with the intention to discredit others. Regrettably, racial history as it is being taught in America's schools and churches includes gaps in information, often layered with disinformation that perpetuates white supremacy in its various forms. Analyzing data and listening to the narratives as told by those who identify with or who are a part of a group being discriminated against can help resist the demoralization resulting from unfair moral judgments and arm citizens with the data needed to stop policy- and lawmakers from implementing and executing the crippling policies and laws that further disadvantage communities that need compassion and opportunity rather than judgment and violence.

To apply the principles and lessons of Scripture properly and effectively to the complex nuances of race and racism in America in the twenty-first century, one must understand histories, the peculiarities of race in America, and the often difficult to identify driving forces of inequity and injustice. Michael Emerson and Christian Smith, in their classic work *Divided by Faith*, contend, "We tend to understand race, racism, and the form of racialization as constants rather than variables."[18] From 1619 to the mid-twentieth century, racism was on full display in the form of overt and blatant symbols such as exclusionary signage (Whites Only), racially discriminatory laws, and segregated neighborhoods, schools, and government entities. The erasure of those symbols, along with the progress we have made as a nation, does not mean that racism no longer exists.

Racism still exists in many insidious and harmful, oppressive ways. As it relates to racism and racial inequities, it is not enough to simply say that slavery and Jim Crow segregationist policies are the foundational reasons that Black communities suffer from a lack of resources and are underdeveloped. White Americans have had greater opportunities to acquire wealth and land and far fewer barriers of economic, lending, and housing discrimination than African Americans. The pulpit and pew must connect the dots and "make it make sense" for people who have been conditioned to measure and qualify racism and racial injustice using measures from the

1950s and 1960s. For example, the preacher's ability—and willingness—to prove how urban ghettos are a product of how "banks discriminated with redlining, refusing to give mortgages to African Americans or extracting unusually severe terms from them with subprime loans . . . and, as a result, many remain concentrated in urban neighborhoods"[19] is just one example. Miguel De La Torre's observation of voter suppression is key here; he correctly argues, "The Voting Rights Act may have passed Congress over half a century ago, but the suppression of votes nullifying its intent went from overt means (asking prospective voters how many jellybeans are in a jar) to covert (demanding voter ID while closing facilities in communities of color at which to obtain the ID)."[20]

Emerson and Smith admit that racial practices that produce racial division in the United States are increasingly covert, are embedded in institutions, avoid direct racial terminology, and are invisible to most whites.[21] If sacred anthropologists cannot explain racism and inequities to those who deny its existence by using the credible experiences of those affected by it and by pointing to reliable data, they will be severely limited in persuading others of these realities.

Consider the Covid-19 pandemic and its deadly effects on Americans of all races. Though the pandemic has taken a toll on every community, an analysis of data reveals that communities of color suffer from the deadly virus in disproportionate numbers, even though such communities are in the minority. The Center for Disease Control reports, "A growing body of research shows that centuries of racism in this country have had a profound and negative impact on communities of color. The COVID-19 pandemic and its disproportionate impact on people from some racial and ethnic groups is a stark example of these enduring health disparities. COVID-19 data shows that Black/African American, Hispanic/Latino, American Indian and Alaska Native persons in the United States experience higher rates of COVID-19-related hospitalization and death compared with non-Hispanic White populations."[22]

The pandemic not only took its toll on the mortality rates of minority communities; for those who survived its deadly onslaught, the pandemic left its mark by revealing significant economic disparities. In the state of

Alabama, residents who earned less than $27,000 per year were severely hurt financially during the pandemic. Alabama Appleseed reports, "We estimate Black workers comprised 25 percent of workers in this quartile but only 19 percent of Alabama's workers. Put simply, Black workers were disproportionately likely to work the exact type of low-paying jobs that evaporated during the pandemic."[23]

How does analyzing data and experiences of individuals serve the sacred anthropologist in examples like this? Just as anthropologists and sociologists use data findings to disprove false and hurtful narratives about communities of color, sacred anthropologists can analyze the data and research made available by respectable scholars, government entities, and nonprofit agencies. In ages past, some of the leading scientists in America developed racial science to disprove the humanity of Black and brown image bearers. These embers are still aflame today.

Among these scientists were Charles Caldwell, Samuel George Morton, Samuel A. Cartwright, George Gliddon, Josiah C. Nott, and Louis Agassiz. They developed and pushed the flawed and racist creation theory of polygenesis, a theory that rejects the most accepted biblical creation argument of humanity having one common ancestor in favor of the position that casts humanity as multiple species, thus having more than one origin and different original ancestors. Terence Keel writes, "This group of scientific men took up a rigorous study of the various human populations across the globe and worked collaboratively to develop the idea that racial variation stemmed from immutable physical differences passed down from one generation to the next, and therefore the races could not have shared an ancestor."[24] The analysis of scientific data is precisely what served to challenge the misinformation and disinformation perpetuated by these respected scientists who helped create racial supremacy and racial hierarchy. These flawed theories would be proven unfavorable and scientifically objectionable by anthropologist Franz Boas and African American sociologist W. E. B. Du Bois. Keel reports that both Du Bois and Boas "argued that it was illegitimate to use the cultural forms of a social group as a proxy for determining their biological worth or evolutionary progress. . . . Boas and

Dubois helped precipitate a paradigm shift in the way scientists visualize the perception of race and ultimately opened the door for more robust critiques of racial determinism and the use of race as a tool of scientific analysis during the remainder of the twentieth century."[25]

The kernels of misinformation and disinformation planted in the past have been nurtured and have grown into contemporary racist myths that often cast Black and brown people as loud, aggressive, violent people who need policing and who are unworthy of the dignity afforded to image bearers. These false images, propped up by misinformation and disinformation, also are one reason voters elect officials that enact "tough on crime legislation" rather than those who advocate for the disbursement of the valuable and deserved resources of which our communities are deprived and so desperately need, such as social services, mental health facilities, quality schools, job opportunities, and healthy food options. When sacred anthropologists analyze the wealth of data, statistics, and information available to us, they can become advocates of fair policies and laws that build communities and empower individuals instead of supporting political candidates who draft and pass laws that further cripple and marginalize the most vulnerable. Fortunately, we need more than Bibles to help us navigate the complexities of sinful racist ideologies and structures.

Pulpit and pew must be armed with the Bible and a deeper understanding of the complex functionalities of race, power, and capitalism in this country. Forensic anthropologists analyze skeletal remains to establish a biological profile, cultural anthropologists analyze data from ethnographic studies, archeologists analyze artifacts from dig sites to determine historic particularities, and sacred anthropologists analyze the truth of the Bible along with the truths gained from the research of other disciplines to better understand the root causes of human suffering and disparities.

Making Amends

In his award-winning essay in the *Atlantic* entitled "The Case for Reparations," Ta-Nehisi Coates explains how from the 1930s to the 1960s, thousands of African American homebuyers in Chicago's North Lawndale community were trapped in predatory home contracts that denied them opportunities to earn equity. In many cases, those trapped in these scams lost their homes after paying thousands in payments collected by the seller/owner, not the bank. By the time many of these citizens fought back through joining the Contract Buyer League, which brought a series of lawsuits, it was too late. As Coates exclaims, "The suit did not win them any remuneration," and "By then they'd been bilked for thousands."[26]

The sacred anthropologist understands that racial reconciliation doesn't end with void and empty apologies, joint worship services, or multicultural church planting, in which the dominant culture often holds the deeds to the building, controls the doctrine, and determines the direction of ministry and resources. Making amends starts with tangible, measurable, quantifiable gestures of contrition and repentance that can be felt by the masses of people whose ancestors and communities have been robbed of potential and resources. It is very difficult to measure the weight and sincerity of apologies, especially when those who apologize for the racial atrocities of the past revert to condoning or, at least, turning a blind eye to political personalities who vow to "make America great again" by returning to the ideologies from whence they claim to apologize. Apologies often turn into insults and cruel taunts and teases when those offering the apology fail to ratify it in the voting booth. Randall Kennedy correctly contends, "Others supported Trump precisely because he is overtly reactionary—'Make America Great Again'—heralding a purported lost glory when gender roles and identities were stable, when Christianity was the unchallenged societal religion, when police malfeasance was patiently accepted, and when an implicit but clear deference to the imagined superiority of whiteness reigned supreme, from immigration policy to television screens, to Miss America pageants, to universities, to Pulitzer Prize awards."[27]

The sacred anthropologist advocates for and makes amends by restoring what has been taken, replacing what has been deprived, recovering what has been lost, and reforming systems that rob humanity of human flourishing. We have the capacity to reform and to change systems and structures radically and fundamentally. Slavery was abolished, Jim Crow was outlawed, and at the time of this writing, several municipalities are changing how they do policing by outlawing choke holds and implementing citizen review boards. Those acts, past and present, are examples of what making amends should look like. The most common concept is reparations. This book is not the place for an exhaustive defense or an examination of the complex topic of reparations, but my point is that vulnerable communities must be extended tangible reparations that will remain long after apologies have been unofficially and silently rescinded by those making the apology. Often, apologies are in lockstep with former egregious behaviors, although under different names. On May 10, 1865, Frederick Douglass, in his speech at the American Anti-Slavery Society, said, "Slavery has been called a great many names, and it will call itself by yet another name; and you and I and all of us had better wait and see what new form the old monster will assume, in what new skin this old snake will come forth next."[28] The sacred anthropologist seeks to lead the church and the state to make amends by demolishing the ideologies that resurrect themselves in different structural manifestations.

Reparations is a call for an economic or monetized restoration. The concept and practice are anchored and cemented in the Hebrew Scriptures (Exod 21:33–22:1; Lev 6:1–7; Num 5:5–8). In the Old Testament, restitution requires the perpetrator to "make full restitution for his wrong" (Num 5:7) and demands additional penalties be paid along with appeals to the priest for atonement. Often our repentance is full-hearted but empty-handed. In their poignant and penetrating book *Reparations: A Christian Call for Repentance and Repair*, Duke L. Kwon and Gregory Thompson make the case for contemporary reparations by confronting the "everybody is dead and gone" excuse that opponents of reparation offer as a way to avoid the reparations discussion. Kwon and Thompson rightly observe, "The guilty party must return what *would have been* the heir's rightful possession by inheritance had its transmission never been interrupted by the theft."[29]

Due to the incalculable wealth lost to slavery and Jim Crow over a 344-year period, economic reparations are just the beginning. I agree with

Kwon and Thompson, who put it this way: "To view White supremacy as a theft of not only wealth but also truth and power provides important insights regarding White supremacy's inner logic. It is also a more accurate amount of White supremacy's devastating cultural reach. To frame the harm done by American White supremacy in exclusive economic terms is actually to obscure the nature and magnitude of that harm. . . . The true imperative of reparations is not simply for a debt to be repaid but for an entire world to be repaired."[30]

Speaking again to the scores of Black people shot and killed by law enforcement, financial settlements were reached with the families of the deceased. However, in most cases, the officer(s) was not charged or prosecuted, and the system responsible for producing the errors and the officers who committed them remains intact. Dionne Smith-Downs's son, James Rivera Jr., was killed by the police on July 22, 2010, at only sixteen years of age, one day before his seventeenth birthday. Ms. Smith-Downs testifies to the emptiness she often felt during the process: "Throughout my settlement conversations, I told them, 'I want justice. I want a trial, not your money. Or you could give me my son back, and I would walk up on out of here.'"[31] The officers responsible for Rivera's death were never prosecuted.[32]

On July 29, 2008, the United States House of Representatives, following the lead of Rep. Steve Cohen (D-TN), apologized to African Americans for the brutal institution of slavery and the subsequent government-sustained Jim Crow. Throughout history, several states, colleges and universities, and corporate businesses have apologized for the 246 years of chattel slavery that took the lives, posterity, opportunities, culture, and wealth of millions of enslaved Africans. Today, most predominantly Black communities in America's cities trail predominantly white communities in economic development, education, and political power. No number of apologies can compensate for the deprivation and dearth created by slavery and Jim Crow.

On July 31, 1966, the National Committee of Negro Churchmen (NCNC), a group of very influential Black churchmen, wrote a document entitled "Black Power" and then published it as a full-page ad in the *New York Times*.[33] The document of July 1966 was signed by forty-eight of the most influential clergy in America and was the beginning of Black clergy claiming the independence of the Black church from white theologians who were either silent about or complicit in the social plight of Black people. The document addressed four groups of people: leaders of America, white churchmen, Negro citizens, and mass media.

To the leaders of America, the document decried the violence against Black communities perpetrated by lynch mobs. They also addressed the abuse of power that often contributes to the manifestation of poverty in urban communities. To the white churchmen, the NCNC called for a true integration and sharing of power among the races, while they also called out the hypocrisy that resides in the white churches. The NCNC sought to empower and encourage Black citizens by calling for unity and collaboration in the use of power to help the masses. They also encouraged Black people to embrace the term *Black power* and to recognize their power and identity while demanding that all Americans do the same. Finally, the document acknowledged the courage that the mass media exhibits when covering the atrocities afflicted upon Black people. The NCNC also warned the media of false truths and pointed to the few voices that could be trusted to interpret the events in America concerning the Negro in a different light. The NCNC urged the mass media to seek out the truth.

These ministers demanded more than an apology. For them, amends meant making things right. Sacred anthropologists in the pulpit and pew walk alongside victims of discrimination and bigotry by advocating for reparations in a variety of forms. For instance, colleges and universities can provide scholarships to minority students and hire more women and racial minority scholars in the fields of religion, theology, and ethics. These schools can also be more equitable in funding minority research projects that center on justice and equity.

Sacred anthropologists can challenge bureaucracy in churches and denominations that tend to shut women and minorities out of leadership positions. Corporate businesses can hire from and make financial investments in communities of color. Municipalities can ensure that infrastructures of lighting, sidewalks, and green space are installed in impoverished communities to deter crime and increase safety and leisure. Sacred anthropologists, as complex and challenging as the task will be, can find a way to build wealth opportunities for minority communities, families, and individuals. All of these things matter to the Triune God whom we worship.

Finally, and most importantly, sacred anthropologists can advocate for amends by joining forces with other people of goodwill to dismantle the legacy of white supremacy and the fortress of systemic injustice that still exists in our nation's institutions. These are the means by which amends will reach the masses, not just those who are already positioned to thrive in a world that remains hostile to people of color.

The sacred anthropologist should pursue racial reconciliation through and by the cross of Jesus Christ. Thus, reconciliation will cost all of us; it demands that we engage in the ministry of reconciliation (2 Cor 5:18–19). Reconciliation is never easy or cheap. Apologies are welcomed, but amends that can be measured in tangible, economic means are necessary. If we continue to offer apologies alone, as sincere and heartfelt as they may be, we will find ourselves decades later repeating the failed attempts at racial reconciliation tactics. The ministry of reconciliation given to sacred anthropologists demands more.

Conclusion: Assisted Advocacy

The last function of the sacred anthropologist is to assist other churches and secular agencies in ministry and activities that intentionally disrupt the philosophies, theologies, and practices that tend to normalize racism and injustice. The sacred anthropologist, in the pulpit and pews, will lead the congregation and community to form sacred partnerships with other churches, individuals, and entities who strive to advance the cause of justice in our nation.

The Black church was at the fore of the civil rights movement. African American pastors and preachers from Prathia Hall to Martin Luther King Jr. and laity from Fannie Lou Hamer to Medgar Evers took the lead in the fight for equality and justice. However, this battle would have never been won decisively if it were not for the sacrifice and moral fortitude of other religious and nonreligious communities. Christians must seize the opportunity to defeat evil by partnering with men and women who love justice and mercy and who are advocating for the same goals.

Partisan politics, territorial theologies, and racial divisions are some of the obstacles to unity and partnership. These are often barriers to unity instead of bridges that allow us to join forces with one another other to triumph over the sins of racism and injustice. Indigenous tribes must unite with the sons and daughters of former slave owners; National Baptists must commit to partnering with African Methodist Episcopal, United Methodist, and Full Gospel Fellowship leaders and laity to develop strategies that will mobilize voters, raise community awareness, and hold public officials accountable. Churches must show up to city council and school board meetings when elected representatives are fighting for their constituents. Politicians should be willing to "cross the aisle" and do what is morally right and ethically upstanding regardless of the fallout and backlash. Foot soldiers of the civil rights movement can assist the energetic and fearless youth of today in their advocacy to bring about measurable change in their communities. The scholars who walk the halls of academia need to tread the streets of urban ghettos and travel down rural roads to gain deeper insights into how a lack of agency affects the everyday lives of people who live with their backs constantly against the wall. Finally, the pulpit must come together with the pew to create ministries that will benefit the least of these in our midst.

Sacred anthropologists *appreciate* other cultures and *analyze* the available data and resources provided through the research and scholarship of scholars and grassroots organizations, as well as the individual experiences of everyday people, while advocating for *amends* that restore economic losses and reform broken systems. We *assist* other congregations and organizations that want to see "justice roll down like waters, and righteousness like an ever-flowing stream" (Amos 5:24).

Social Crisis Preaching

A Rhetoric of Resistance

THE GREEN MILE is an award-winning film starring Tom Hanks as Paul Edgecomb, a death row prison guard, and Michael Clarke Duncan as John Coffee, a Black death row inmate awaiting execution in a Louisiana prison for raping and killing two young white girls, a crime he did not commit. After witnessing John's spiritual powers, Paul and the other guards realize that John is innocent of the crimes of which he has been convicted but is nevertheless trapped in a racist criminal justice system in the Deep South that shows little regard for Black lives. In a very poignant scene, two days before Paul is to escort John down "the green mile" to the death chamber, he and John discuss the condemned man's last wishes:

John: Hello, boss.
Paul: Hello, John. I guess you know we're coming down to it now.
    Another couple of days. Is there anything special you want to eat
    for dinner that night? They can rustle you up almost anything.
John: Meat loaf be nice. Mashed taters, gravy. Okra. Maybe some
    of that fine corn bread your missus make, if she don't mind.
Paul: Now, uh . . . what about a preacher? Somebody to say a little
    prayer over you?
John: Don't want no preacher. You can say a prayer if you like.
Paul: Me? Suppose I could if it came to it.

I have often wondered why John Coffee decided he "don't want no preacher" praying over him. In the Deep South, John Coffee was another innocent victim of racial injustice who died without agency or advocacy from anyone, including the church. I soon realized that the reason Coffee refused to have a preacher present was because he understood that vocal prison guards are more sacred than voiceless preachers. What could possibly cause the prisoner to devalue the voice of the herald of the gospel? What could possibly cause someone to favor the secular over the sacred, the prison guard over the preacher? Where were the preachers in John Coffee's situation? Why weren't there churches and Christians advocating for John Coffee? Why did he distrust the church and preachers? I believe that scene in *The Green Mile* sends an important message to the church. When those who are *called* to speak out and advocate for justice allow systems of injustice to exist unchallenged, those who are affected by injustice will seek presence and voice from other sources. The second revelation of that scene sheds light on why we have a profound level of distrust in the church. Distrust of the church is exacerbated when those who are trusted to carry out the ethical requirements of the faith fail to do so.

Preaching is one of sacred anthropology's most important tools. I define social crisis preaching as *biblically rooted, Spirit-enabled proclamation that develops and drives congregations to compassionately care for and radically confront social crises in the communities where their neighbors live, work, worship, and play.* The goal of social crisis preaching is to *intentionally develop congregations that care about the social crises in their neighbors' communities and confront them using the power of the Holy Spirit.*

The focus on our "neighbors' communities" is key to social crisis preaching and encourages congregations to follow Christ's exhortation to "love your neighbor as yourself" (Mark 12:31). It also acknowledges that "crisis" means something different to each congregation. Some congregations do not necessarily face the plights that plague their less fortunate neighbors. In their communities, crime rates are low, schools do not struggle for funding, job opportunities abound, water is clean, healthy food is readily available, and the police serve and protect the public. In situations like this, blessings and privilege should be a green light to deny yourself, take up your cross, and follow Christ (Matt 16:24). I do not mean to suggest that affluent congregations do not have their own problems but that those problems do not rise to the level of crisis. Still, they must care about the crises that affect their neighbors.

The focus on "their neighbor's community" prevents congregations from cherry-picking which problems they serve and from attempting to qualify and define what those crises should and should not be. When social crisis preaching is aimed at guiding congregations to care about and confront the social crises in their neighbor's community in the power of the Holy Spirit, they begin to see the *other* as community, and compassion is transformed into redemptive acts of love that disrupt and disturb the perpetual cycles of disenfranchisement and pain that too often mar the lives of image bearers.

The term *social crisis preaching* is most associated with Kelly Miller Smith Sr., the celebrated civil rights icon and late pastor of First Baptist Church, Capitol Hill, in Nashville, Tennessee. Smith introduced the term in a 1983 Lyman Beecher Lecture at Yale Divinity School entitled "Social Crisis Preaching."[1] Smith defines social crisis preaching as "the proclamation of that which is crucially relevant within the context of the Christian gospel in times of social upheaval and stress."[2] My definition and description of social crisis preaching build upon the foundation that Smith has laid.

I was first introduced to Smith's work by Robert Smith Jr., my preaching professor in the MDiv program at Samford University's Beeson Divinity School. I have always thought of myself as a student of the history of the Black church and its involvement in the civil rights movement. However, I must admit that prior to my final semester at Beeson, I had never heard of Kelly Miller Smith Sr., his thirty-plus-year ministry in Nashville at First Baptist Capitol Hill, or his standing as one of the most prolific and distinguished preachers in America. Smith was one of only thirteen African Americans to have been invited to deliver the prestigious Lyman Beecher Lecture at Yale University.[3] Additionally, in 1954, *Ebony* named Smith one of the ten most outstanding preachers in America.[4] Dr. Robert Smith Jr. suggested that I might be interested in pursuing a PhD and that Kelly Smith Sr. might be a good research subject. Indeed, as I learned more about Smith, I became enamored of his life, ministry, and preaching. Smith's work has shaped my own preaching, encouraging me to be more intentional. I hope to continue Smith's work by adapting his concept of social crisis preaching so that it might be more effective in a contemporary context.[5]

Social Crisis Preaching as Embodied Practice

Social crisis preaching is not a solely intellectual endeavor that can be learned and taught in the classroom. To engage in effective social crisis preaching, one must go out into the world and experience the pain of communities afflicted by social crises. Preachers who are born in the crux of society's crises and who witness the perpetual frustration and humiliation of societies underserved and are called to "sit where they sat" embrace the irresistible urge to confront the ghost of the past and the haunting spirits of injustice in the present. Kelly Miller Smith Sr. experienced social crisis firsthand in his hometown of Mound Bayou, Mississippi, and that knowledge greatly impacted his life to the extent that Smith's story can be said to be the story of Mound Bayou. Smith knew the threat of violence upon the Black community. In many of his sermons, he spoke out against mob violence, as many preachers in the South were constantly compelled to do. Smith knew that racial violence and white supremacy knew no boundaries, and it did not distinguish between Black professionals or those who worked in the fields or in homes. His personal embodied experience with the threat of violence enabled him to connect with his audiences who faced these same threats. For example, biographer Peter Paris emphasizes what pain sharing meant to Smith in Mound Bayou through an encounter with the lynch mobs of Mississippi: "Raised in the all-black town of Mound Bayou, Miss. Smith had little experience with the whites until a gun-toting lynch mob roared into town when he was twelve. The mob threatened to shoot a black doctor whom they suspected of treating the man they were chasing.

As young Smith watched, the doctor defied them: 'Well shoot.' The would-be lynchers drifted away."[6]

The Mississippi Delta where Smith was raised also knew one of the most vicious acts of racial violence in the history of our nation. Mound Bayou is in Bolivar County, Mississippi, a mere forty-four miles from Money, Mississippi, the town where fourteen-year-old Emmett Till was snatched from the home of his sixty-four-year-old uncle in the middle of the night on August 28, 1955, and brutally murdered in an act of extrajudicial violence.[7] The Till murder and other acts of racial injustice and unfairness fueled Smith's passion and responsibility for social crisis preaching.

Prophetic Preaching

Several terms are often used to describe preaching that aims to address social crisis: *political preaching, preaching on social issues, civic preaching, preaching on racial issues, just preaching*, and *prophetic preaching*, among others. Insightfully, André Resner Jr.'s comments about "just preaching" are similar in aim and purpose to social crisis preaching. Resner offers, "*Just preaching* is a deliberate redressing of the preaching task from the perspective of justice. Why justice? Because it has been and continues to be the greatest social need in human, but also divine, history. A faith driven by the biblical vision realizes that a world that continues to compromise fair treatment of human beings based on color, ethnicity, or socioeconomic status that God, and all of God's creation, is being compromised at the same time."[8] However, of all the terms used to delineate proclamation that leverages the word of God against social crises, I find *prophetic preaching* the most apt in capturing the telos of social crisis preaching.

The tradition of biblical prophetic preaching comes from the Old Testament prophets. The God-inspired oracles of the prophets warned the nation of Israel to conform to Yahweh's vision. As Willem A. VanGemeren notes, prophetic preaching strongly correlates with crisis: "The prophets spoke God's word to people in crisis. During war, siege, famine, or other adverse times, they addressed living people and applied God's message to the issues at hand."[9] Prophetic preaching in the church should always beckon the people of God to conform to God's vision for humanity in light of the redemptive work and grace of Christ.

VanGemeren states, "Through the prophets, people heard the 'voice' of God and received a new vision for life. . . . The prophet viewed human activities from God's vantage point."[10] The proclamation of God's vision calls for our nationalistic visions to take subservient roles to God's vision for *all*, regardless of earthly divisions. The competing myopic visions, dreams, and nostalgic reflections that summon people to "take back" or to return to an era of cultural dominance conflict with God's vision for humanity. Any vision or dream, regardless of how exotic and grand in imagination, that does not include the reign of God in Christian ethics and spirit must be questioned and addressed. Prophetic preaching is the constant call of the preacher to confront people with the imperative to "choose this day who you will serve" (Josh 24:15).

Prophetic preaching confronts and ultimately rejects the visions, mores, theologies, and narratives constructed in hierarchic and homogeneous silos that lead to the discrimination and oppression of disenfranchised minority groups. More akin to the American dream than John's vision of the coming kingdom of God, these cultural narratives are normative and dominant in secular society and are often pervasive in the American churches. I agree that prophetic radicalism is the rejection of what Otis Moss describes as "the existential tragedy manufactured by a false anthropology and demented theology"[11] espoused by American culture and often preached in white churches. The prophetic preacher offers the oppressed and the oppressor a different reality: an alternate vision, community, and identity. Walter Brueggemann insists, "Prophetic utterance is offered in circumstances dictated by dominant imagination but is utterance that contradicts what is taken for granted. Such imagination refuses to accept accepted explanations for present circumstances."[12]

The telos of prophetic preaching is the reconciliation that takes place between the community of the afflicted and justice and peace. This occurs

when congregations become disciples who disrupt the ideologies and practices that shape the minds of those responsible for injustice. Since the community of the afflicted is composed of those for whom justice and peace
have been limited and restricted, this reconciliation arises from the result
of confronting, exposing, and ultimately dismantling the root causes of
spiritual malady and social malfeasance.

When does prophetic preaching become radical, and what defines
radicalism? Prophetic preaching becomes radical when it strikes at the root
of social crises. Radicalism comes from the word *radix*, meaning "root."
Prophetic radicalism exposes and uncovers the root causes of social crises.
The social crisis preacher does not settle for utopian fantasies of multiracial
communities, nor does the preacher rest on halfhearted apologies void of
truth and righteous justice. The social crisis preacher biblically exposes the
flawed theologies, oppressive politics, economic disparities, and personal
sins at the roots of social crises and heals and extends conciliation to divided
and fractured parties. The effectiveness of prophetic preaching cannot be
measured with decibel markers nor with the thermometer of emotional
enthusiasm. Prophetic radicalism can be as powerful in a whisper as in a
thunderous roar; it can be as moving in the facial expression of streaming
tears as in a grimacing scowl. Like prophetic preaching, social crisis preaching speaks truth to power and the powerless. It addresses sin in all forms.
As we will see below, social crisis preaching aims to disrupt the societal ills
that have brought many communities to a crisis point.

Elements of Social Crisis Preaching

This chapter will focus on the three distinct elements of social crisis preaching that comprise the sacred anthropologist's arsenal: the descriptive use
of language, interdisciplinary content, and pastoral courage. These three
elements of social crisis preaching mirror, respectively, Aristotle's
three modes of persuasion: pathos, logos, and ethos. This similarity between
effective preaching and ancient rhetoric is no surprise, since all preaching aims to persuade listeners to believe in the saving power of God and

convince them to adopt a life modeled after the ethics of Christ's earthly life. As we will see below, social crisis preaching's persuasion focuses on social convictions, aiming to alter divisive political climates by introducing possibilities that foster unity and equity and by disrupting false narratives that bind the oppressor and the oppressed.

In ancient, classical Greek rhetoric, the orator's rhetorical acumen was measured by his possession and utility of ethos, logos, and pathos. The rhetor's ethos was a testament to moral fiber and perceived character, while logos had to do with logic and the speaker's ability to reason, and finally, pathos was measured by the orator's passion and emotional appeal. As Aristotle explains, "Since proofs are affected by these means, it is evident that, to be able to grasp them, a man must be capable of logical reasoning, of studying characters and the virtues, and thirdly the emotions—the nature and character of each, its origin, and the manner in which it is produced."[13]

Social crisis preaching, much like Greco-Roman rhetoric, is concerned with persuading the listener. Unlike Greco-Roman oration, social crisis preaching acknowledges that Christian proclamation is a work of the Spirit; therefore, the source of the social crisis sermon is the Bible, and the power behind the speech act of social crisis preaching is the Holy Spirit and not simply eloquence of words (1 Cor 2:1–5). In social crisis preaching, persuasion is a result of the hearer being transformed by the Holy Spirit. Thus, logos, ethos, and pathos are induced by the Spirit and are tools that can be used to encourage the hearer to embrace God's redemptive purpose for humanity. Finally, social crisis preaching, like all Christian preaching, should be a call to action and application. As Kelly Miller Smith poignantly wrote, "Social crisis preaching aims at eliciting a response. In traditional evangelical terms it is preaching for a decision, indeed, for a decision for Christ."[14] Here, "a decision for Christ" means embracing the ethical example of Christ as One who defends the poor, challenges and critiques social and ecclesial structures, and disrupts the forces of death and oppression. Persuasion for the sole purpose of converting believers ignores issues of injustice and is silent against the rising tides of secularism, exploitive capitalism, and religious nationalism. Social crisis preaching aims to develop congregations that will disrupt any ideology and practice that is contrary to God's redemptive vision for humanity.

In this chapter, I am seeking to provide a tangible representation of the sacred anthropologist and how preaching fulfills the characteristics of that calling. The preaching and ministry of Kelly Miller Smith serve as a model for sacred anthropology and social crisis preaching in particular.

THE DESCRIPTIVE USE OF LANGUAGE

All preaching involves language—that is, choosing one's words to convey a specific message. In social crisis preaching, however, the precision of language is especially important. In the words of Kelly Miller Smith, "The preacher has the awesome responsibility of using words to proclaim the Word of God. Words are at times imprecise and freighted with meanings contrary to what may be intended."[15]

Quintilian writes in *Institutio Oratoria* that "to speak well is indeed the orator's business, but the science of speaking well will still be rhetoric."[16] Preachers use precise words to communicate the gospel's claims on injustice. To move the congregation to care about and confront the crises in their community, preachers must speak well. Speaking well is not simply a cerebral exercise; it also involves a connection with those who are affected by injustice—passion produced by pain. Of the three modes of persuasion, pathos registers passion in the speaker and stirs passion in the hearer with words.

The word *crisis* implies urgency. Therefore, it should be assumed that verbal articulation in social crisis preaching will be passionate. Crisis requires passion, not passivity. Kelly Miller Smith's life and sermons are a paradigmatic representation of courage—a manifest model of what Kenyatta R. Gilbert refers to as "a deep prophetic consciousness."[17] God provides then levies the restlessness and burden felt by the prophet to address social crises in accordance with methods that match God's character and God's vision for God's people. Whether it is Moses's burning desire to represent Yahweh for his people against an evil Egyptian empire, Isaiah's spiritual motivation to speak on the behalf of the poor, or Nehemiah's troubling concern about the spiritual, economic, and political state of his nation, prophets acquire an irresistible righteous urge to speak truth to power (Exod 3:1–12; Isa 61:1; Neh 1:1–5; 2:1–5). For Smith, social crisis preaching did not stem from words used in wrath or rage. As he wrote, "Words in the form of mere angry rhetoric or incendiary verbalization do not constitute social crisis preaching."[18] In social crisis preaching, carefully placed words spoken in the right tone can communicate the severity of the crises being addressed, thus persuading the hearers to commit to being agents of redemptive change.

When the preacher's words are flat, dry, or passionless, the preacher may very well fail to convince his audience that there even *is* a crisis. Social crisis preaching requires language that can both make theological language comprehensible to laypeople and connect it to real-world contexts. However, information without inspiration rarely moves listeners to embrace causes that often call for enormous sacrifice. The descriptive use of language in social crisis preaching serves three major functions in the social crisis sermon:

1. to give voice to the pain experience of people beset by injustice, unfairness, and social crisis by the preacher, who is a part of the community of the afflicted;
2. to articulate the pain and lament of God as One who also shares in the pain of God's people; and
3. to remind people to hope in God as the only remedy and response to social crisis.

Giving Voice through Sharing Pain

The pastor must be not only a part of the body of Christ but a member of the community. Like Ezekiel, the preacher must sit where they sit and walk through the agony with the community of the afflicted as they experience delayed and denied justice (Ezek 3:15). In his sermon "A Look at Ourselves," based on 2 Corinthians 13:5, Smith's words reflect the visceral experience of a pastor who has shared the pain of his community: "Sometimes patriotism keeps us from looking at ourselves as a nation. Suppose

America looked at herself for what she really is. Sometimes our zeal for justice as bruised victims blinds us to the need for our looking at ourselves as black people in this land."[19]

Effective preaching does not merely observe people suffering, stand by abstractly, or conduct personal interviews where people are asked to describe their pain. It can only be accomplished when the preacher lives incarnationally with the people who sat in the pews. In the African American church, call and response is one indicator that the preacher is describing the unique and particular agonies of the people in the pew. In the call and response dynamic, the preacher's words are met with "amen," "tell it," "thank you Lord," "you preaching," and "use him Lord," to name a few of the expressions that affirm the resonance of the preacher's words in the listeners' lives.

The preacher who has sat with parents of incarcerated children can describe the gnawing feelings of hopelessness and the mentally draining anxiety of being without legal recourse in a justice system that has a history of treating the poor as less than. During the sermonic event, carefully selected words drawn from the well of incarnational pastoral work can give voice to the parents' frustration. The preacher cannot borrow the pain or the words; they must own both. James Henry Harris describes this reality within the context of Black preachers and Black communities: "Preaching in silent pain is at once a metaphor and an irony, two literary terms surrounded by the philosophical and the medicinal. It is a double-sided irony because while silence presumes speech, preaching is not presumption. It is speech personified, embodied speech, yet it is not without its own silence. By this I mean that preaching is a testimony to silence, and particularly a testimony. To pain and to suffering in the Black community. It is a crying out, a yelling and screaming, if necessary, in response to Black people's pain and suffering."[20]

Preaching is painful. Not only because the preacher must enter the painful experiences of the people to appropriately articulate with words how *the* Word provides remedy and response to suffering, but because the sermonic act is delivered from the pain of preparation. As a mother carries and then experiences the pain and joy of delivery, so the preacher cannot escape pain as a perpetual piece of the process that ends in joy. James Earl Massey referred to preaching as a "burdensome joy." It is one of the oddities of life that experiencing pain seems to produce uniquely expressive, moving poetry.

The beauty of African American preaching lies in the inspiration of poetic language and rhetoric that comes from the experience of sharing pain. As Cleophus LaRue states, the "traditional black church expects and appreciates rhetorical flair and highly poetic language in the preaching of the gospel."[21] The poetic use of language is not limited to the learned and educated. It does not fit into the category of an acquired skill. The poetic use of language is inherent in the painful experiences and grief that come from being a member of a threatened and terrorized community. Pain produces poetry. Consider the painful poetry of Paul Laurence Dunbar:

> A crust of bread and a corner to sleep in,
> A minute to smile and an hour to weep in,
> A pint of joy to a peck of trouble,
> And never a laugh but the moans come double;
> And that's life!
> A crust and a corner that love makes precious,
> With a smile to warm and the tears to refresh us;
> And joy seems sweeter when cares come after,
> And a moan is the finest of foils for laughter;
> And that's life![22]

Or how Langston Hughes describes the life suffering of a mother as she articulates her experience to her son in metaphoric language in his poem "Mother to Son":

> Well, son, I'll tell you:
> Life for me ain't been no crystal stair.
> It's had tacks in it,

And splinters,
And boards torn up,
And places with no carpet on the floor-
Bare.
But all the time
I'se been a-climbing' on,
And reaching landin's,
And turning corners,
And sometimes goin' in the dark
Where there ain't been no light.
So boy, don't you turn back.
Don't you set down on the steps
'Cause you finds it's kinder hard.
Don't you fall now-
For I'se still goin' honey,
I'se still climbin',
And life for me ain't been no crystal stair.[23]

These poems are blood turned to ink. The beauty of poetry is found in the blessing and burden of the painful experiences borne by the prophet-poet as a member of the community of the afflicted.

The poetic rhetoric of the prophet-poet is often the paint that fills the tabula rasa of the unmoved and numb minds who live in a world where painkillers serve as coping mechanisms. Poetic language is language used *by* the hurting to speak *to* the hurting. In her book *The Humblest May Stand Forth*, Jacqueline Bacon argues "that oppression serves as an impetus for formation of an oratorical style."[24] Bacon suggests that there is a correlation between the pain in oppressive experiences and rhetorical ingenuity.

Historically, the Black preacher has functioned as both prophet and poet, and language allows those unaccustomed to suffering to be inwardly touched. The poetic use of language allows for the prophet-poet as a member of the community of the afflicted to descriptively express the pain of the community in words that point to hope.

Communicating the Pain of God with Words

In an era of prosperity gospel preaching, there is not enough lament in the sermon. Lament is an outward expression of pain that the Triune God registers on the soul of his people. Social crisis preaching also communicates the pain the living God experiences when systems and structures diverge from God's ordained purpose and will, thus producing people who wreak havoc on other people and communities through economic, social, and ecclesial injustice. That's why the Black preacher and Black congregation would cry out in call and response through their testimony, "He's a burden bearer and a heavy load sharer." The sacred anthropologist, then, is a wounded healer, who serves as a conduit who communicates the pain of God to the people of God.

Each time a George Zimmerman, a Kyle Rittenhouse, or a Darren Wilson is allowed to evade justice, God is in pain. Each time a Derek Chauvin is convicted, God's heart is broken because the soul of one who bears God's image has been distorted and unrealized. Whether there is conviction or acquittal, God's heart is broken over the very system that produces and promotes the mentality of white supremacist violence. Social preaching gives voice to the pain experienced by God and those who are created in the image of God but often suffer from a world that has been diverted from God's plan of redemption and restoration.

Jesus embodied the word he preached, but he also shared in the pain and suffering that was a result of the human predicament. He has "borne our griefs and carried our sorrows" (Isa 53:4), and he is able to sympathize with our weakness (Heb 4:15). Sharing pain is not only sharing in the pain of the people; the preacher must share and communicate God's pain. Preachers have a responsibility not only to speak into the pain of the afflicted but to join our congregation in their pain and suffering.

The effectiveness of social crisis preaching stems from the hearer knowing that a representative from the community of the afflicted understands the fear, anxiety, and weight of daily burdens and that they can communicate the medicinal power of the word of God about One who has borne our sorrow and carried our grief. The Black church could sing, "Jesus knows all about our struggles, He will guide til the day is done: There's not a Friend like the lowly Jesus: No, not one! No, not one!" Then in another song entitled "I Must Tell Jesus," they would sing, "I must tell Jesus all of my trouble, I cannot bear these burdens alone, in my distress He kindly will help me, He ever cares and loves His own."[25] African American preachers from every era know this. In the words of Cleophus LaRue, "Seasoned pastors from an earlier generation could often be heard admonishing younger ministers not to be afraid to 'preach a little.' Such encouragement was intended to free the poet in the preacher and allow the presence of God through the power of language to lift the sermon to higher heights."[26]

Passion born of pain is a major element in social crisis preaching and the social crisis sermon. The preacher who embodies the pain of the people also embodies the hope of the people. Therefore, the preacher articulates hope as precisely and passionately as they articulate pain. The preacher's words need not end in pain but rather rest in joy, for in the joy of the Lord lies the strength to endure the long pain of injustice.

Preaching Words of Hope

A patient in pain feels a certain level of confidence in a doctor who can describe the physical discomfort of their patients with pinpoint accuracy. When the doctor can use the right words to describe the patient's pain—when they feel it and can adequately articulate how it makes them feel—trust is gained and hope for relief is expected. If the patient trusts the diagnosis, they will trust the prognosis. So it is that when the sacred anthropologist uses descriptive language in the social crisis sermon, the hearer will also trust that they know the answer to social ills. When social crisis preaching can describe the heartbreak God experiences whenever we dispense justice to the highest bidder, trust is gained. When the social crisis preacher can communicate the fear that elder members feel when they live in a drug-infested community or a war zone, those members will trust the social crisis preacher pointing them to the only true hope in the world: Jesus.

James Earl Massey explains how the African American preaching tradition of which Smith was a part is anchored in a homiletic of hope. Massey states, "The concern for freedom justice, love, and hope is reflected on nearly every page of Scripture; not to see this when the Bible is read is to miss what is most germane for life as God intended it."[27] Not only does social crisis preaching aim to promote hope amid the pain of God and the pain of the people; it also celebrates as a result of the hope of justice.

INTERDISCIPLINARY CONTENT

Pathos is defined as "passion" and therefore signals urgency. Logos, or the rational and logical aspects of the sermon, uses interdisciplinary content. In this way, the social crisis sermon is supported by factual evidence that makes the preacher's argument credible. Passion spoken in generalities or in broad brush strokes can be irresponsible. Preaching in this manner can be interpreted as condescending and accusatory. The social crisis preacher cannot assume that every person within their congregation agrees that racism is systemic or that the criminal justice system is flawed and disenfranchises minority communities. The preacher must show these realities by using objective data, real-life experience, and witness testimony to establish statements that would otherwise be dismissed or rendered fallible. Interdisciplinary content can be grounded in facts of history, political science, truths of medicine, statistics of racial and economic disparities, and other undisputed data. The preacher can provide historical and contemporary examples of structural injustice and systematic inequities in the sermon that will shine a fluorescent light on the evil that lurks within the dark corners of our sometimes oppressive society. Social crisis preaching must transcend the preaching of personal opinions, political preferences, cultural presuppositions, and popularly accepted ideologies of racism and injustice.

The social crisis sermon is infused with statistics, data, culture, history, science, political theory, notes from last week's city council meeting, the results of the last census, and philosophical musings, to name a few of the interdisciplinary subjects that are used to bolster the theological claims spoken from the word of God. None of these subject areas are the source of the social crisis sermon, but they are used to support the biblical argument that the preacher wages on behalf of the biblical text. Sacred anthropologists respect science and data as God's truth. Sacred anthropology understands that the various disciplines within interdisciplinary content are indicators that reveal how far humanity has strayed from God's plan.

Assistant professor of preaching and worship at Lexington Theological Seminary Leah Schade is known as the eco-preacher. She often engages in crisis preaching regarding creation and consistently depends on interdisciplinary content such as environmental data and statistics provided by agencies and institutions like NASA, Georgia Institute of Technology, and ecotheologians to support her theological arguments for Christians being good stewards of creation. Schade employs and defines terms such as *deoxygenation, phytoplankton,* and the earth's "bloodstream" in her writing and preaching to make the case that "climate change is affecting health, families, national security, and our food supply, to name just a few impacts. Earth's body and our bodies are connected. It's past time to care about both."[28]

From early 2019 to the present time, the global pandemic Covid-19 has wreaked havoc on our world. At the time of this writing, in the United States alone, there have been 47,916,623 cases of Covid-19 and over a mind-boggling eight hundred thousand deaths. The Covid-19 pandemic constitutes a social crisis. Oddly, the church has been a major battleground of the public's perception of the deadly virus and how the Christian community has responded to it. Relying on conspiracy theories and irresponsible theological arguments, various churches have been responsible for the spread of the virus, thus resulting in the deaths of members.[29] Pastors in some of these churches have forbidden facemasks, encouraged handshaking, and defied social distancing mandates despite CDC, state, and local mandates.[30] Some pastors have used weak theological arguments, citing fear and a lack of faith if church members wear masks, receive the Covid vaccine, or elect not to attend corporate worship services.

Social crisis preachers during the pandemic have relied heavily on data and research from the scientific and medical communities to refute conspiracy theories and half-truths concerning Covid-19. Moreover, these pastors have bolstered their sermons with social crisis ministries, which include hosting Covid-19 testing and vaccination opportunities for the community. In addition, pastors have armed themselves with data from their state and local hospitals to govern restrictions on in-person worship. In these cases, preachers who use interdisciplinary content in their sermons to inform their members of how Covid-19 is affecting their community are engaged in saving the lives of their members, and thus they are agents who participate in the redemptive purposes of God.

When sacred anthropologists use data to sustain life, the word of God must be brought to bear on the complex issues of the moment. Interdisciplinary content in the form of data, statistics, historical patterns, and cultural insights also contributes to the fact that God, through Jesus, is concerned about the social conditions of creation.[31] Ronald Allen suggests, "If the Christian community is to make an adequate witness to God's unconditional love and call for justice in respect to social issues, the preacher needs to engage in frequent conscientious reflection on them."[32] Preaching that is applicable is preaching that guides the hearer to apply the word of God to concrete realities in our politically and socially divided world.

In African American churches, the teaching pulpit often corrects the errors of the classroom by teaching the excluded facts of history teachers. Members of Black churches are often taught a version of US history hidden from the students who attend America's schools. It is a version that fills in the gaps between the capture of the enslaved on the shores of Africa and the Civil War and the gap between the Civil War and the civil rights movement. Nikole Hannah-Jones, in her most anticipated work, states,

> This history rendered Black Americans, Black people on all earth, inconsequential at best, invisible at worst. We appeared only where unavoidable: slavery was mentioned briefly in the chapter on this nation's most deadly war, and then Black people disappeared again for a full century, until magically reappearing as Martin Luther King, Jr. gave a speech about a dream. This quantum leap served to wrap the

Black experience up in a few paragraphs and a tidy bow, never really explaining *why*, one hundred years after the abolition of slavery, King had to lead the March on Washington in the first place.[33]

In my own preaching, whether before Black audiences, white audiences, or multicultural congregations, I seize the opportunity to reteach history by using, as an illustration, a narrative from history, told from the perspective of the enslaved or the Indigenous to right the errors of history told the wrong way. I am convinced that the teaching and telling of false narratives of history is one of the symptoms of racial sin sickness in America, thus largely responsible for the contemporary racial division in this country. In Smith's baccalaureate sermon at Tennessee A & I State University, he employs statistics and data from a Gallup Poll to underscore how the sentiments of Northern and Southern whites toward integrated neighborhoods have an economic impact on Black families. Smith explains,

> In employment in housing and even in public accommodations to some extent, the segregationist turn of mind is quite evident. You perhaps read the Gallup Poll Report on the attitudes of white parents towards having their children attend schools with Negroes. When asked how they would feel about having their children attend schools with more than 50 percent of the students colored, 60 percent of the Northern parents said they would object, and 62 percent of the Southern parents would oppose the arrangement. Three years ago, in response the same question, 86 percent of Northern parents would object. On the surface, it appears that the South is getting better and the North is getting worse! The point, however, is that it is tragic that in any part of the country there are those who have such unenlightened attitudes towards persons merely because of the color of their skin.[34]

This use of interdisciplinary content shows the sociological relevance of Smith's theological claims. Interdisciplinary content provided to the hearer through objective data and reliable sources will undergird theological claims in the social crisis sermon, which will, in turn, broaden and deepen our faith in the areas where we are often shallow.

Examples abound of preachers who masterfully weaved scientific data, statistics, and the political and social arguments at their disposal into their social crisis sermons. William Sloan Coffin's understanding of legislation and its effects on the powerless, when he speaks of the welfare reform bill, referred to at the time as the Personal Responsibility Act, in a sermon entitled "The Politics of Compassion," is one example. Confronting the evils of white supremacy, Martin Luther King Jr., in his notable sermon "The Drum Major Instinct," touches on economics, international policy, and philosophy as some of the interdisciplinary content of the sermon.[35] In Prathia Hall's sermon "A Nightmare in Broad Daylight," she eloquently gives commentary on women's roles in freedom struggles throughout US history, percentages of literacy rates among children, contemporary cultural inequality, and Black folk religious practices.[36] The sermons of Howard John Wesley, Leslie Callahan, Freddie Haynes, Sally Brown, Lenora Tubbs, Charlie Dates, and Will Willimon, to name a few of the preachers who engage in social crisis preaching, reveal preachers who have a firm grasp on capitalism, international policy, government, law, US history, and ethics.

The use of interdisciplinary subjects in the social crisis sermon is a way of showing the relevance of Scripture and allowing the Scripture to shine its light in the corners of our world where injustice hides in plain sight. Likewise, interdisciplinary content used in this way provides objective, indisputable evidence that uncovers the lies that politicians sometimes use to keep the innocent at bay until the ink is dry on policies that cause further disenfranchisement among marginalized communities. Kelly Miller Smith understood the importance of respecting hearers enough to provide theological and sociological information from other disciplines to enlighten the congregation for the cause of liberation. Forrest E. Harris Sr. notes that "Smith's leadership was informed by a keen theological mind that understood the relationship between religious experience and political awareness. . . . The theological and practical wisdom that shaped Smith's ecclesiology and guided his liberation praxis contributed to the development of collective and critical consciousness at a crucial period in the city of Nashville."[37]

Cultural barriers make empathy among races almost impossible. Where there is no empathy, there is usually a dismissal of the crisis altogether or a denial that people's experiences are real. It is difficult for non-Black communities to understand the real fear of racial profiling, the constant threat of police brutality, and the claims that the criminal justice system is against them. The preacher needs objective data to make the case. Social crisis preaching exposes these systemic evils by not only making claims but supporting the claims. In myriad ways, from police brutality to mass incarceration, to disenfranchisement in voting, to poverty, and to fatherless homes, African American communities suffer at the hands of an overcriminalized justice system. Sermons dealing with sin and the love of neighbor that cite these disparities will aim to move hearers to redemptive action by voting for candidates who are morally and politically motivated to bring about change. For instance, though the United States has only 5 percent of the world's human population, it has 25 percent of the world's prison population.[38] The imprisonment rate of Black adults at the end of 2019 was five times that of white adults, despite African Americans being only 14 percent of the US population.[39] And Black males aged eighteen and nineteen were twelve times more likely to go to prison than white males in the same age range. Historically, racist attempts to portray African Americans as immoral and criminal or as vagrants were enforced through legal instruments such as the Fugitive Slave Act, Black Codes, convict leasing, and Jim Crow laws.[40]

The statistics above raise ethical issues about justice and how image bearers are viewed and treated. Some would insist that this data reveals a decline in the traditional family unit and points to a lack of personal responsibility rather than systemic inequities. While there may be some validity to the statement that the alleged breakdown in the traditional family unit is the reason for high incarceration rates among African American adults, these very statistics also reveal that mass incarceration and overcriminalization are some of the main contributors to fatherless homes and breakdowns in the familial unit in African American communities.

In an age where communities are becoming increasingly polarized, preachers must use interdisciplinary content in the sermon as servants to the word of God to foster unity and reveal the urgent need for the church to intentionally care about and confront the social crises in their neighbor's community in the power of the Holy Spirit.

PASTORAL COURAGE

In Greco-Roman rhetoric, ethos is reflected in the perceived character of the speaker. For social crisis preachers engaged in sacred anthropology, pastoral courage is the medium by which the social crisis ministry is carried out. The weight of social crisis preaching is brought to bear through the pastor's engagement with their congregation. Put simply, pastors earn the right to be prophetic. Kelly Miller Smith counts pre-proclamation functionality as a component of the social crisis sermon. In this insightful pastoral advice, Smith argues that the social crisis sermon begins before the preacher mounts the pulpit or utters a word from the sacred rostrum. Pre-proclamation functionality is the preacher's involvement in social issues, their knowledge of social crisis, and their participation in the communal affairs that affect their members. A younger generation would say this means "having skin in the game." When preachers are perceived to be ethical, moral, and the embodiment of integrity, their sermons on social crises have weight, and they are more likely to persuade their congregation and the communities to the side of the liberating God who saves through Jesus Christ.

In 1955, Smith joined twelve other Black parents in filing a class action lawsuit intended to force the Nashville Board of Education to enforce the noted Supreme Court's *Brown v. Board of Education* decision to desegregate public schools.[41] Although this act of fatherly and pastoral courage did not result in the immediate integration of the public schools in Nashville, it did start the process, resulting in Smith's daughter being one of the first Black children to integrate Nashville's public school system in 1957. Pastoral courage can only be exhibited as pastors live incarnationally with those they are called to serve. The power of the preacher's social crisis sermon is felt through the minister's courage outside the pulpit. Pastoral courage is a part of social crisis praxis whereby preachers are more equipped to deliver effective application in the sermon through reflection upon the courageous acts of social crisis ministry.

I have found in my own social crisis ministry and preaching that pastoral courage is not only exercised when facing political authorities; pastors are also called to exhibit courage when facing denominational and ecclesial leadership. Social crisis preaching exposes evil in any system. Institutional loyalty seeks to preserve the institution, not free individuals. There are myriad examples of how prophetic leaders have been forced to break free of the religious strongholds constructed by denominational loyalists to move progressively forward in the cause of justice and liberation for the masses. Pastoral courage is sometimes a call to confront the majority within religious and civil institutions, from Jesus confronting moneychangers in the temple (Matt 21:12–13), to Perpetua standing firm against martyr-making Septimius Severus and the Roman Empire, to William Tyndale's resolve to place the English Bible in the hands of the commoners, to Martin Luther's courageous attempts to reform the Catholic church, to the Baptist Foreign Mission Board denying overtures from the Alabama Convention allowing slaveholders to be missionaries, up to the twenty-first century, where the courage of William Barber and Traci Blackmon is displayed in the fight for voting rights.

A Mosaic Model of Courage

Courage is a characterization of the African American prophetic preaching tradition that is most assuredly drawn from the historical identification of the Black preacher with the Old Testament prophet Moses and from African Americans' identification with the oppressed Israelites. Herbert Robinson Marbury states, "For most African Americans, the Bible's stories, particularly exodus, grounded their religious knowledge. African Americans readily transferred its themes of bondage and freedom to their own context."[42]

In this Mosaic model, courage is exemplified in the virtues of self-denial and sacrifice. Another profound example of Smith's pastoral courage is his willingness to forgo the personal accruements and luxuries that mark the almost celebrity status of preachers who lead large churches.

In 1963, Smith was called to become the pastor of one of the largest African American churches in the country, Antioch Baptist Church in Cleveland, Ohio. However, after only three months, Smith sensed that his work in Nashville was not complete, and since First Baptist Church, Capitol Hill, had not yet chosen a successor for Smith, according to John Britton, they "voted to re-call their beloved minister, with only about 25 objections out of over 250 voting."[43] Smith's love for his Nashville church and the unfinished business of racial reconciliation in Nashville explains why, as Britton states, "Rev. Kelly Miller Smith, of the distinguished Mound Bayou, Miss. Smiths, was about to turn his back on a rich prestigious Cleveland Baptist Church to return to the much smaller congregation, First Baptist."[44] Pastoral courage in this case is anchored in pastoral love. There is an inescapable call to serve people in the power of the Spirit to which the pastor is compelled to obey. It requires profound courage to live against the tide of conventional norms for the sake of a purpose and a people to which God has called.

Richard Lischer, James T., and Alice Mead Cleland, professor emeritus of preaching at Duke Divinity School, comment, "African Americans have traditionally decorated their leaders with messianic imagery and have given 'Black Moses' to such figures as Harriet Tubman, Booker T. Washington, Marcus Garvey, Joe Louis, Martin Luther King, Jr., Jesse Jackson, and many others."[45] Henry H. Mitchell, African American church historian and the first Martin Luther King Jr. professor of Black church studies at Colgate Rochester Divinity School, also testifies, "Exposed in depth to the Old Testament, the slaves found it amazingly similar to their traditional faith. . . . They understood well the tale of Exodus and devised a spiritual song to celebrate it ('Go Down, Moses')."[46] Rhonda Robinson Thomas adds, "By appropriating the Exodus story, Afro-Atlantic people posited themselves as protagonists in a major narrative of the New World filled with communities where the Bible functioned as the single most important centering object for social identity and orientation among European dominants."[47] Pastoral courage is the ethical responsibility and requirement of servant leaders who are called to engage the church beyond the act of preaching.

Spirit-Governed Courage: Power Sharing[48]

Here, Spirit-governed courage is measured by the social crisis preacher's willingness to share power and leadership due to self-control and commitment to the greater good. I pause here to mention one of the Achilles' heels of the civil rights movement. The male-dominated movement often denied power sharing and leadership to capable and able women. Women such as Fannie Lou Hamer and Prathia Hall had to create their own spaces in this majority male movement. Courtney Pace says of Hall, "A man with her talents and successes would have been a nationally recognized civil rights leader, held a prestigious pulpit, and served as president of a major denomination. That path was not open to Hall, despite the influence she held."[49] Fannie Lou Hamer chose to serve with mentor Ella Baker and the Student Nonviolent Coordinating Committee (SNCC) rather than the more popular Southern Christian Leadership Conference (SCLC) after Baker "parted ways with the group in 1960 over their leadership model. Like many civil rights organizations of the period, SCLC built the organization around one central (male) leader, mirroring the leadership of Black churches."[50] Hamer, realizing the limitations placed on Black women within the movement, according to Keisha N. Blain, "denounced what she viewed as a paternalistic impulse among certain NAACP leaders who often attempted to dictate instructions that followed the line of respectability rather than allowing local people to carve out their own paths to achieving civil rights."[51]

Smith was a proponent for women in leadership in the 1950s and '60s when most Black churches and Black pastors maintained a complementarian outlook in the home, the church, and the civil rights movement. This mindset underscored his courage amid many of his friends and colleagues and served to underscore that he, like Hamer, "believed that focusing on one leader—or even a few—proved detrimental to social justice movements."[52] Perhaps the most notable advocacy for Black women sharing power in the church and the civil rights movement with their male counterparts is the scholarly work of Evelyn Brooks Higginbotham. Higginbotham gives a defense for the much debated "respectability politics" as the means by which women should forge their "fight" for equality within ecclesial ranks. Higginbotham states, "Male-based traditions and rules of decorum sought to mute women's voices and accentuate their subordinate status vis-à-vis men."[53] That Smith mentored many women, including Diane Nash, is a testament to the courage he exhibited in sharing power.

Smith's courage embodied the Spirit's fruit of self-control (Gal 5:23), and his radical proclamation was in "wedding the radical offensiveness of his stand for rights with the reasonableness of peaceful means."[54] Spirit-governed courage is often reflected in temperament and the preacher's willingness and ability to negotiate with parties of contrasting views on social issues to the end that such negotiations do not compromise the non-negotiable elements of justice and liberation.

Some well-meaning church leaders lack the courage to deny themselves by being open to sharing power and leadership for the greater good. Leila Meier testifies to Smith Sr.'s openness to power sharing:

> The sharing of power was another component of Smith's leadership style which set him apart and contributed to the fidelity which he inspired. He did not seem to conduct himself as a man who coveted authority; he was more likely than not to give credit to others for achievements in which he himself had played a central role. This attribute made him a natural leader among clergymen, who recognized that he would never consciously abuse his influence and power. The congregation of First Baptist and Nashville's other supports of civil rights likewise appreciated his qualities of humility, integrity, and generosity, all which intensifies his attraction as a moral example and trustworthy chieftain.[55]

In the popular "Who Speaks for the Negro?" interviews with Robert Penn Warren, Smith discussed his role as chairman of the Negotiations Committee for the sit-ins in Nashville during the 1960s and how much the negotiations called for self-control. Herein lies a clear example of how the fruit of the Spirit is applied in negotiations for social justice:

> We needed someone who would not "blow his top" so to speak. When something is said that everybody knows is wrong, you say okay, we don't accept it. But if you become emotional about it, then we would render ourselves useless, in going further. So somehow, we had to learn that certain people could not be used for this but could be used in another area. . . . This is an aspect of it, that is much more strenuous and significant, than many people seem to think. It's less dramatic but it's a tremendous thing, to sit there with a group of people who come from two entirely different worlds. You don't speak the same language and they perhaps have never seen Negroes close up except as janitors and maids, never talked across the table on an equal level, you got to overcome this kind of barrier.[56]

The relevance of Smith's comments in this interview to social crisis preaching has to do with the pre-proclamation functionality of the social crisis preacher. Pre-proclamation functionality, as defined by Smith, measures "what the function of the preacher has been prior to the crisis proclamation."[57] Spirit-governed courage *outside* of the pulpit, which is manifest in the fruit of self-control, is imperative for the impact of Spirit-governed courage *in* the pulpit. Spirit-governed courage is a distinct and evident dynamic in Smith's social crisis proclamation.

Pastoral Courage and Jesus Christ

The social crisis preacher, though dealing with rudeness and wrath, presents a radical message of justice and reconciliation while advocating for a

Christ-centered peace—a peace that, according to Smith, only emanates from Christ. Smith exhibits this trait in his sermon "The Way of Christ," taken from John 14:6, where he proclaims,

> The way of Christ is the way of peace. When we speak of peace our minds automatically lead us to a consideration of world peace. Yes, the Christ way is certainly capable of restoring peace and order in the world. But, as imminently important as world peace is when our consideration of the peace problem ends on the world-wide basis, it hasn't gone far enough. Too often we concern ourselves so much with things far away that we neglect the things near at hand. There is a type of peace which the world needs which is dependent upon the way of life you and I choose. . . . It is a peace that destroys that group prejudice which makes a mockery of our so-called American Democracy and American Christianity. What is this way of Christ that introduces this type of peace to us? That answer is simple—the Christ way of peace is the way of love and understanding.[58]

In the crux of social crisis and blatant racism, Smith possessed perpetual courage and advocated courageously for peace by maintaining composure and never allowing anger and bitterness to take root in his heart and become an ingredient in his sermons.

Courage in social crisis preaching calls congregations to intentionally care about and confront the social crisis in their neighbor's community. In his sermon "The Story of Jesus," Smith repeatedly calls attention to the courage of Christ while challenging his hearers to adopt courage as a means of dealing with social crises. In this sermon, as Smith points out, Jesus is an exemplar of courage and the radical example of confronting injustice through courage:

> A second appealing feature about the story of Jesus was the courage and moral heroism exhibited by him. All the world loves a hero;

Jesus was a Hero in every true sense of the word. Then he said, "I am meek and lowly in heart," none of the adversities and oppositions of his life proved him a coward. Jesus was rejected by his townsmen, deserted by friends, and crucified by his enemies, but through it all He has remained the Great Moral Hero of all times. When ridiculed and scorned by religious authorities Jesus remained calm and undisturbed. . . . Even in the face of merciless death on the cross—when he was mocked, scorned and spat upon—the garden of courage, well cultivated in the soul of Jesus exhibited the fragrant flower of love, for it was in love, born of moral courage that Jesus prayed, "Father forgive them, for they know not what they do."[59]

Courage is required of preachers who lead congregations to model Christ's example as agents who disrupt the accepted norms of injustice.

Courage in Truth Telling

Courage is speaking truth. Like the prophets who spoke boldly to the powerful and the whole people, social crisis preaching comes from the awareness that, according to LaRue, "to keep silent and refuse to speak the truth is to deny ourselves a meaningful contribution to the human situation."[60] Courage was the one trait that the Old Testament prophet employed to unmask idolatry, expose ungodly tyranny, and call out injustice. This bold truth-telling can put the speaker in the line of fire; for example, God reminds the prophet Jeremiah to have courage: "Do not be afraid of them" (Jer 1:8); "Do not be dismayed by them" (Jer 1:17).

Courage is the undeniable trait in Smith's social crisis preaching, which requires that the truth be spoken at all costs. Courage cuts through the morass of myths, half-truths, and impotent solutions to get to the root of injustices and declare in sermonic expression, "You will know the truth, and the truth will set you free" (John 8:32). Regardless of consequence and risk, the African American pulpit is one of courage, where the preacher is a truth-teller. Cleophus J. LaRue states, "Truth is active and dynamic; it requires a personal relationship with the one who is Truth."[61]

Smith did not dodge political issues in his sermons, nor did he allow them to become the focus of his proclamation by overshadowing the gospel. Unlike many secular critics and some Christian critics of America, Smith did not alienate his hearers into racial factions or into politically opposed tribes. Smith was a Christian who loved his country, and like a true prophet of God, out of that love, he spoke against her sins. He did not absolve himself from the shortcomings of America by levying the responsibility of reconciliation and healing on the dominant population alone. From 1 Chronicles 16:29, Smith demonstrates this shared ownership in his sermon "Beauty" by proclaiming, "The trouble is that the heart of America is badly in need of being decorated with the beauty of holiness. Before these troubles of ours are overcome, we must work on the heart of America. And the heart of America is your heart and mine."[62]

Smith's prophetic radicality explores the impact of the Christian faith on social conditions. The social crisis preacher of courage, often without political allies, financial undergirding, or institutional resources, faces the powerful among foe and friend alike, and like the prophet, they are given grace to "be not afraid of them, nor be afraid of their words" (Ezek 2:6).

Conclusion

Social crisis preaching, with its roots in the Old Testament prophets, closely aligns with the prophetic tradition of the African American preaching tradition. Both are *Spirit-inspired, Christian proclamation anchored in the revelation of God's word regarding redemptive justice as God's response to social crisis.* Faithfulness to the practice of social crisis preaching is designed to *intentionally guide congregations to care about and confront the social crises in their neighbor's community in the power of the Holy Spirit.* Out of this definition and description flow the distinctive rhetorical elements of social crisis preaching, like the modes of persuasion found in Greco-Roman rhetoric—pathos, logos, and ethos. The respective parallels to this in social crisis preaching are descriptive language, interdisciplinary content, and pastoral courage.

In his recent and widely acclaimed book *Shoutin' in the Fire: An American Epistle*, Danté Stewart tells of attending a church around the time of Alton Sterling's murder by the Baton Rouge Police Department on July 5, 2016. Stewart details the frustration that many African Americans who attend predominately white or multicultural churches feel when national news of police brutality or some other injustice or atrocity faces the Black community, and there is never a lament nor a call to confront the social crisis in the neighbor's community from the pulpit. Stewart recalls that a sermon series about marriage started the week after Sterling's death and that "we were being taught, week in and week out, how to be Christian. But we were not being taught how to live in America."[63] Social crisis preaching teaches congregations to live as citizens of redemptive love in America as we await our inheritance in that celestial country where social crisis will be no more.

Old Scars, New Wounds

Suffering as a Spirituality for Prophetic Radicalism

PROPHETIC RADICALISM IS, in its varying forms and methods, inseparable from the fight for social justice within the context of the Christian church. By definition, prophetic radicalism is Christian proclamation and living that *expose* the root causes of injustice while *advocating* for God's redemptive justice and simultaneously *acting* as agents of disruption in accord with the life and ministry of Christ through the power of the Holy Spirit.[1] Thus, the African American church, based on a sense of spiritual conviction and vocational calling, has felt the inexorable responsibility to engage in the life-sustaining and freedom-extending acts of social justice activism through prophetic radicalism. It has never been easy, and many who engage in the work of prophetic radicalism in the quest for social justice are wounded in the process. The awareness of such wounding has led Christians to fashion a Christian spirituality that draws from personal and collective spiritual disciplines needed to sustain those engaged in prophetic radicalism in the pursuit of social justice.

Christian spirituality is born from wounds that are associated with following the way of the cross-bearing Savior, who defeated evil through and by the cross. We say with Paul, "I bear in my body the marks of Jesus" (Gal 6:17). For the Christian, social justice activism is an indirect means of following Christ. Christians who pursue Christ, the kingdom of God, and God's righteousness (Matt 6:33; Phil 3:12–16; 2 Tim 2:22) as their ultimate goal distinguish Christian activism from activism that makes justice the end of their pursuit. Because we are in constant pursuit of Christ, likewise, we consistently pursue justice along the way. In this pursuit, woundedness is inevitable.

Old scars and new wounds point to our present sufferings caused by the reemergence and replaying of the same injustices of yesteryear. Voter disenfranchisement, police brutality, gerrymandering, rampant crime, family dysfunction, and poverty can best be described as recycled pain due to battles fought long ago. The battles for justice are often won, but ultimate victory will only be realized when Jesus, "destroying every rule and every authority and power," has "put all his enemies under his feet" (1 Cor 15:24–25). These battles were won in large part because the Christians who led the battle were sustained by a faith that was fueled and refueled by forgiveness, prayer, and the singing of spirituals that articulated both their suffering and hope, coupled with corporate suffering that united them with Christ, the suffering and liberating Savior.

While we must acknowledge the powerful activism of secular advocates and those who are not connected to faith, church, or Christian spirituality, Christian social justice activism aims to bring glory to the God of justice and is thereby empowered and enabled by the presence of God's abiding Spirit. While people create and manipulate policies and other systemic and structural mechanisms that are often responsible for the oppression of communities, it is also true that "we do not wrestle against flesh and blood, but against the rulers, against the authorities, against the cosmic powers over this present darkness, against the spiritual forces of evil in the heavenly places" (Eph 6:12). Thus, we remember, "the weapons of our warfare are not of the flesh but have divine power to destroy strongholds" (2 Cor 10:4), so we "take up the whole armor of God, that [we] may be able to withstand in the evil day" (Eph 6:13). This is the inherent power that is available through Christian spirituality.

What is *social* justice? The term is ambiguous and often left to be defined by a myriad of interpreters. James P. Hanigan of Duquesne University gives a very concrete definition and description:

Social justice . . . looks to the legal, political, economic, and social forms—one should also add the ecclesial forms—within which we live and which establish rights and obligations, demands possibilities within the total framework of existence. Social justice seeks out the proper framework of structural relationships that provide individuals and groups with more or less space in which to act and which to foster or impede the development of such ability as they have to act. At the most formal level social justice is concerned to provide both individuals and groups with their due measure of the opportunity to act and the ability to act, to build structures that will honor and enlarge the dignity of the human person.[2]

Social justice activism is unavoidable and inevitable for those who are most faithful to Christianity. This truth is centered in the acknowledgment that Christianity is a practical religion. Philip Jacob Spener comments, "The rule in human life is, *Qui proficit in literis & deficit in moribus, plus deficit quam proficit*, that is, whoever grows in learning and declines in morals is on the decrease rather that the increase. This is even more valid in spiritual life, for since theology is a practical discipline."[3]

Two of the world's leading spiritual intellectuals of the twentieth century, Martin Luther King Jr. and Dietrich Bonhoeffer, saw social activism as an essential aspect of Christian life. Bonhoeffer and King both maintained that the church cannot turn away from the world and that to do so would likely result in grave moral confusion.[4] The proof of Christian fidelity is as much public as it is private. Orthodoxy's worth lies in orthopraxis.

Though depressed, dispossessed, and disinherited, African Americans conjured the spiritual resources to withstand and even triumph over social injustice. This spiritual tenacity speaks to an undeniable and identifiable spirituality. This statement is not to dismiss, overlook, or underappreciate the individuals and groups who were not Christians and who, at varying points in American history, contributed significantly to the dismantling of bigotry and oppression through social justice activism. Neither can the African American church claim superior status in Christendom. However, as Otis Moss Jr. writes, "[the Black church]'s unique position in this country forced it to see America from the underside and engage the love ethic of Christ as a community bruised and scorned by a society claiming democratic ideals."[5] In this country, African Americans have been an enslaved, disenfranchised, often terrorized, and discriminated-against people. Only their sheer faith in God, expressed through their powerful spirituality, ensured survival and social advancement.

How do Christians sustain the hardships of prophetic radicalism while remaining free of hate and bitterness? How can we engage the evils of our world and not be overcome by them? There must be a spirituality that undergirds and sustains the sometimes heartbreaking, backbreaking, mentally exhausting, and spiritually depleting work of prophetic radicalism in the quest for social justice. The answer to these questions lies in the fact that African American social justice activists were convinced that "the spirituality of African Americans expresses a hands-on, down-to-earth belief that God saw them as human beings created in God's own image and likeness and intended them to be a free people."[6]

Social Justice Activism Requires a Christian Spirituality

The work of social activism demands a spirituality that is robust and firm enough to sustain activism amid evil and structurally oppressive forces: "African American spirituality is a result of the encounter of a particular people with their God. It is their response to God's action in their history in ways that reveal to them the meaning of God and that provided them with an understanding of themselves as beings created by God."[7] An African American Christian spirituality adds depth, meaning, and a spiritual purpose to the work of social justice activism. It also provides the means by which activism can be carried out in a particular context. A spirituality keeps improper motives in check and weeds out individuals who are seeking self-aggrandizement. A Christian spirituality ensures that activism is not self-destructive nor leads to broken and injurious relationships along the way, thus, prioritizing worship of the Triune God as a consistent and necessary practice in the life of activists. Bryant Myers, drawing from Matthew 26 and the woman who anointed Jesus with oil, maintains that Jesus and Jesus alone must be the object of the activist's worship:

> There is an important lesson here for Christians who do relief and development work among the poor. Too many Christian activists are ruining their health and destroying their families while justifying the zeal because of their commitment to the poor. In the name of the poor, activist workaholics suffer from poor health and burnout, and they damage their spouses and children. This is not a gospel stance. This is not what Jesus asks us to do. Our devotion must be directed at Jesus, not the poor themselves. While we certainly are supposed to love our neighbor, especially our poor neighbor, we are to worship only Jesus. The woman understood this and the disciples did not. Getting your spirituality and worship right is key to sustaining one's service to God and the poor.[8]

One must not confuse spirituality with theology. Hanigan notes, "Moral theology can tell me about the central importance of the virtues, the fundamental obligation to obey my conscience, the norms . . . but it cannot tell me how to do any of these things concretely. For this I need a spirituality."[9] For activists working under the constant threat of evil, a spirituality was needed. Hanigan continues,

> A spirituality is a means to an end. It is not an end in itself. No matter what form of spirituality one adopts or attempts to live, one does so, not for the sake of the spirituality itself, but in the hope that this particular means or form of spirituality will lead one to the goal—a goal which Christians describe as union with God, as being transformed into the likeness of Christ, as putting on the mind of Christ, as being led by the Spirit. It is a goal which Christian faith doctrinally affirms in the

language as of salvation, sanctification, and more recently, liberation. To commit oneself to a spirituality is to commit oneself to a method or a means, to a process to a way of life.[10]

The forces that produce injustice are supernatural, and the forces that must contend with the evils that produce injustice must likewise be supernatural. African American Christian social activists understood that effective activism would entail more than intellectual muscle, massive numbers, and political alliances. One could not withstand the powerful, oppressive, supernatural forces of evil without being grounded and propelled by a power greater than human strength and willpower. For Paul, to engage in this spiritual warfare, the Christian was required to "take the helmet of salvation, and the sword of the Spirit, which is the word of God, praying at all times in the Spirit, with all prayer and supplication" (Eph 6:17–18).

The practical spirituality of African Americans, intentionally lived out through the spiritual disciplines of individual and corporate prayer, preaching, and practicing community, were the ingredients of a spirituality that glorified God amid suffering and intense social justice activism.

New Wounds

June 17, 2015, will be eternally etched in the memory of Americans as the date of one of the most atrocious acts of domestic terror in history. This demonic demonstration of violence was a new wound reminiscent of the old scars of our painful past. Dylann Roof, a self-proclaimed white supremacist, vowed to start a race war, and Emanuel African Methodist Episcopal Church was his Fort Sumter.[11] Dylann Roof's murderous acts probed at an old scar, causing a new wound to the soul of American Christians who have tried to heal the nation of the sickness caused by barbaric acts of racism and white supremacy. The fact that this act of terrorism happened to nine Christians who were studying the Bible late in the evening at Emanuel African Methodist Episcopal Church—often referred to as Mother Emanuel—in Charleston, South Carolina, is more telling than it appears on the surface. Mother Emanuel's history is marked by scars and wounds that are emblematic of the Christian faith. These scars and wounds are reminders of our responsibility to bear in our body the marks of Christ (Gal 6:17) *and* of the power of the Spirit to heal the wounds suffered through our cross-bearing witness as agents of disruption and disturbance. Old scars of yesterday's suffering also remind us how we move past the hurt of new wounds.

To practice prophetic radicalism is to accept physical and mental wounds. It is also the willingness to wear the scars. Ironically, and perhaps paradoxically, nonviolent resistance is also referred to as the "fight" for equality. Most fights produce wounds and create scars that remain long after the fight is over. Those who have fought for civil rights have been willing to be wounded. We remember John Lewis's cracked skull on the Edmund Pettus Bridge; Fannie Lou Hamer's brutally beaten body in the jail of Winona, Mississippi; the emotional and mental trauma experienced by Carolyn Maull McKinstry, who survived the Sixteenth Street Baptist Church bombing in Birmingham, Alabama; the calloused feet of hundreds of Montgomery, Alabama, citizens who walked to work for 381 days; and thousands of other people of every ethnicity who have borne mental and physical wounds in the "fight" for civil rights. Some wounds are mortal. The deaths of Martin Luther King Jr., Malcolm X, Jimmie Lee Jackson, James Chaney, Andrew Goodman, and Michael Schwerner were deep blows to the civil rights movement, and the scars left in their wake are permanent. Wounds stem from fighting the good fight. A scar is a constant reminder of the joy that springs from victory. It's not that we want the pain that caused the scar, but in this life in which suffering is a perpetual reality, scars will result—mental, emotional, and even physical scars. Scars can be a source of encouragement and can be worn proudly, as a mother wears the scar of her C-section, with honor, pride, and love. Some wounds are worth our willingness to endure, and the scars are reminders that we will endure.

Mother Emanuel church was born out of the wounds of rejection and the scars caused by state and local regulations that sought to stifle freedom of worship. The Methodist Church of the early nineteenth century limited the freedom and participation of its African members. As a result, Richard Allen led several members out of Saint George's Methodist Church to later establish the African Episcopal Church, the oldest African American denomination. Rev. Morris Brown seceded from the Methodist Church in Charleston, South Carolina, for the same reasons and set out to join the movement started by Allen. This exodus led to the establishment of the Hempstead congregation, a body of believers that included the charismatic slave revolt leader Denmark Vesey. After Vesey's foiled insurrection of 1822, Charleston's white majority imposed strict anti-Black laws designed to prevent the movement and meeting of African churches. Amid these tight restrictions, an underground movement of African Christians continued to meet, and a membership of three thousand emerged to establish what is now Emanuel African Methodist Episcopal Church on September 6, 1865.

This church has been a bastion of resistance and freedom for over 150 years. This ability to resist injustice and promote freedom is sustained by a spirituality that responds to those responsible for its wounds with love and forgiveness. The nation, and perhaps the church, was amazed to see the families of the murdered Charleston nine forgive Dylann Roof. This act of forgiveness gained the praise of President Barack Obama and other civic and church leaders across the nation.[12] However shocking it was to people outside the African American church that forgiveness would be the logical step in healing and moving forward, for those steeped in the African American Christian tradition, forgiveness is a spiritual trait that allows one to heal and maintain one's quest for justice and reconciliation.

Forgiveness as Spirituality

Peter Paris writes, "African peoples have always known the great toll that hatred takes on both the personality of individuals and the life of the community. In the interest of their highest goal, community, they have shunned hatred by cultivating the virtue of forgiveness through the habitual exercise of kindness."[13] The families of the Charleston nine are not the only people who have been scarred by the heinous acts of others but have chosen for-giveness as the path to healing. On September 6, 2018, Botham Jean was shot and killed inside his apartment by Amber Guyger, an off-duty Dallas police officer. Guyger, a white female police officer, claimed to have mistaken Jean's apartment for her own. Mistaking Jean as an intruder, she fired her weapon, ending Jean's life. In a Dallas courtroom on October 2, 2019, the day after Guyger was found guilty of murder, Brandt Jean, the younger brother of Botham Jean, told the court that he had forgiven Guyger. He then looked to the judge and said, "I don't know if this is possible, but can I give her a hug, please?" After the judge gave approval for Brandt Jean to approach Guyger, Brandt Jean proceeded forward and embraced a seem-ingly regretful Guyger.[14]

For churches that engage in prophetic radicalism, suffering is inevitable, so a spirituality of forgiveness is imperative. The spirituality of forgiveness serves as a source of healing and as motivation to continue the fight for justice. The Christian mandate to love and forgive has served as the pri-mary source of strength of the Black church, enabling sustained progress in the battle for justice and liberation. Without a collective spirituality of forgiveness during painful eras of oppression, peaceful activism would turn to anger, attempts to reconcile would turn to plans to retaliate, and efforts to heal would be replaced by strategies to pursue harm and hurt. Unforgiveness halts progress. Bitterness stemming from injustice is a burden and weight that Christians in every era must unload to run their leg of the race toward justice and freedom.

Forgiveness is rooted in altruistic love, and in the face of evil, it has manifested in nonviolent direct action. In the words of Martin Luther King Jr., "Nonviolence is the answer to the crucial political and moral question of our time—the need for mankind to overcome oppression and violence without resorting to violence and oppression."[15] Nonviolence loves the violent neighbor and resists becoming like them, with the hopes of transforming the neighbor through love. Love is more radical than any evil act. Love cannot be overcome by evil, and forgiveness is intrinsically bound to it. Of this spirituality shared by King and people of every ethnicity who believed in its power during the civil rights era, Luther D. Ivory states, "The demands of love in the revolutionary situation brought a moral obligation for noncooperation with the evils of injustice and cooperation with good."[16]

Forgiveness as Self-Care and Self-Love

Forgiveness is a misunderstood practice. For some, it is given too quickly, without critical reflection or responsible thought. Timothy P. Jackson states, "Forgiveness is neither a passive remission of punishment premised on a blind verdict of acquittal, nor a contractual agreement cannily designed to make us more peaceful or cooperative."[17] In some cases, individuals who extend forgiveness still possess a boiling rage. Forgiveness becomes a means of coping with the unbearable pain that they most often know will never be soothed. A growing populace believes that forgiveness thwarts real justice, devalues Black life, allows the perpetrators to escape the full weight of due justice, and permits atrocities to be viewed as single and random incidents of violence instead of a collective disregard for Black life undergirded by systems that devalue the worth of Black and brown experiences. Roxanne Gay's article in the *New York Times* entitled "Why I Can't Forgive Dylann Roof" echoes the sentiments of many: "Black people forgive because we need to survive. We have to forgive time and time again while racism continues to thrive. We have had to forgive slavery, segregation, Jim Crow laws, lynching, inequity in every realm, mass incarceration, voter disenfranchisement, inadequate representation in popular culture, microaggressions and more. We forgive and forgive and forgive and those who trespass against us continue to trespass against us."[18]

Gay's thoughts on forgiveness are not easy to dismiss, but the alternative is "too heavy a weight to bear." Gay's statement "black people forgive because we need to survive" has a dual meaning. Choosing violence by engaging in a race war is a battle that will be lost before it begins. Violence can never become the Christian way. So rather than responding to these injustices by declaring and waging war, thus risking cultural annihilation, we forgive and live to fight another day, month, year, decade. On the other hand, this survival simply means that forgiveness is the most daring, courageous, and self-interested action a person or people can leverage against the perpetrators of violence.

Forgiveness *is* self-care. Forgiveness is self-love. Forgiveness is a step toward mental health. Forgiveness is healing oneself. Forgiveness is transformative. Jackson powerfully asserts, "Although forgiveness wills the good for the wrongdoer, forgiveness can also be the final declaration of independence from the wrongdoer. It refuses to be conformed to and thus controlled by his or her sin, and this refusal is liberation from hatred, resentment, anxiety, and other crippling emotions that lead to despair and vendetta."[19]

Forgiveness is the internal working of God manifest in external gestures toward those who may not realize that they too are human, made in the image of God. When a people forgives, they are refusing to allow the strong forces of violence and systematic dehumanization to disfigure the image of God in them. Choosing to forgive puts us on the beautiful path of love, which leads to peace, rather than choosing bitterness and hate, which lead us to a path of mental turmoil, bitterness, and loneliness. Forgiveness is choosing to be human. This Christian act is the supreme act of self-control, the refusal to take the bait of bitterness that will only lead to a slow and eventually joyless death. Forgiveness is a way of choosing to join God in defining our own lives rather than turning that power over to the person, people, and actions that wounded us and caused permanent scarring. Forgiveness is strength, not weakness.

Private Forgiveness and Public Justice

After being found guilty of Botham Jean's murder and sentenced to ten years in prison, and after receiving public forgiveness from Brandt Jean and public consolation from Judge Tammy Kemp, Amber Guyger and her attorneys filed two appeals.[20] For Botham Jean's mother, these appeals opened a new wound. Jean's mother, a devout Christian, is a remarkable model for Christians who have been wounded by weapons of injustice. We should take away three things from Allison Jean's Christian example.

First, she demonstrates that forgiveness is a personal matter. She remarked after the trial, "There are many Christians who asked me if I would forgive Amber. I will leave my forgiveness for Amber to myself. God knows my heart."[21] While Allison Jean praised her son Brandt for his choice to publicly forgive Guyger, she also refused to allow the public to pressure her into making forgiveness the normal, easy response of Black people, when private pain is also a collective wound. Forgiveness should be a personal matter between the individual, God, and the person who trespasses against us. While there is certainly no sin in informing the public that you have forgiven a violent perpetrator, there is certainly no requirement to make your forgiveness known to the world—or to the perpetrator, for that matter.

Public forgiveness has the potential to minimize the public's perception of the severity of the injury. When forgiveness is announced publicly, there is also the chance that our collective wounds will be ignored and our screams for reform will be seen as crying wolf. Fleming Rutledge insists, "A policy of 'forgive and forget' can produce lasting harm on the political level as well as the personal. Peace without justice is an illusory peace that sets the stage for vengeful behavior later."[22] Forgiveness is not the "get out of jail free" card that some hope it is. The question must be raised, "How does my public announcement of forgiveness serve the collective fight for justice?" Public announcements of forgiveness need not send the message that justice is not expected and required. Public announcements of forgiveness need not absolve racist terrorists from the consequences of their crimes, and they must not imply that the hurts caused by injustice have subsided. Allison Jean reported that "she has had difficulty working, sleeping, and eating and has been worried about her youngest son, who 'doesn't speak much' anymore."[23] In matters of racial violence and injustice, our personal injuries also mean collective wounds.

Allison Jean's wisdom to practice her spirituality in private devotion is a lesson for twenty-first-century Christians who believe that every act must be posted on social media or communicated through a media outlet to be valid. Allison Jean is a disrupter. She refused to allow anyone to dictate how she processed her pain, and she did not allow the unrealistic timetable of public opinion to force her into irresponsible injury to her already broken spirit. Nadine Collier, the daughter of seventy-year-old Ethel Lance, who was one of the Charleston nine, publicly voiced her forgiveness of Dylann Roof two days after Lance was murdered at Emanuel AME.

When people try to live up to the expectation of immediate forgiveness, forgiving becomes a cheap way of coping with grief and pain and an escape from confronting the strong forces of evil behind our injury. Jackson states, "Critical judgers, on the other hand, worry that unconditional forgiveness sacrifices justice on the altar of a bogus charity. A purely unmerited forgiveness abandons standards for responsible action in favor of a 'cheap grace' (Bonhoeffer) that gives free rein to villainy."[24] When forgiveness is extended, it should be an action that stems from faith in the One who demonstrated forgiveness to the degree that no other human would ever have to do. To forgive is an act of obedience motivated by faith in God, who forgives us and commands us to forgive others.

Second, Allison Jean personally practiced forgiveness but publicly fought for justice. In the days following her son's murder, well into the postverdict, Allison Jean decried the horrendous acts of the Dallas Police Department in their handling of the case. Allison Jean called attention to the corruption in the Dallas Police Department, the favoritism shown toward Guyger at the scene of the crime, and the mishandling of evidence. After the verdict, Allison Jean cried:

> "What you saw and what you heard in the courtroom really showed what your system is, and you must seek to do something about it," she said. "You saw a contaminated crime scene; you saw deletion of evidence by persons in high offices. You saw turning off of body cams and saw cameras in the vehicles. You saw investigations that were marred with corruption and throughout the trial what I kept saying

to myself is, 'Botham was a child of God and we know he did not deserve what he got.' The most hurtful part is for me that even after he was shot, he was left to die."[25]

This is the responsible rhetoric of love, anger, and communal responsibility. Allison Jean understood the Christian responsibility to forgive in order to heal, but she also would not allow injustice to remain unscathed in Dallas. Her love extended beyond *her son* to the sons of every member of the Dallas community by exposing the evil that causes mothers to grieve.

The tension between forgiveness and justice is a topic that scholars have wrestled with for centuries.[26] Forgiveness can coexist with justice. Forgiveness releases our perpetrators from our wrath and ceases the pursuit of revenge and retribution, but forgiveness does not get in the way of justice. While we forgive, we should remember that justice is also a Christian virtue. Fleming Rutledge argues, "Forgiveness must be understood in its relationship to justice if the Christian gospel is to be allowed its full scope."[27] In the case of unrepentant and repeat offenders, seeking justice also may save others from experiencing the trauma that we endure because of selfless acts of violence or injustice.

While forgiveness creates a world where compassion lives, justice creates a world where evil ceases to rule. We should hold people accountable for their actions while releasing them from death wishes, hateful grudges, and forms of disrespect and ill-treatment. Amber Guyger was sentenced to ten years in prison rather than the twenty-eight recommended by the prosecutor. Botham Jean's mother has filed a lawsuit against Guyger and the city of Dallas and called for police training requirements. Allison Jean commented after the sentencing "that 10 years in prison is 10 years for her reflection, and for her to change her life. But there is much more to be done by the city of Dallas, the corruption that we saw during this process must stop, and it must stop for you . . . and it must stop for everyone."[28]

Third, forgiveness extends release to the offender while it considers the communities most at risk of being trespassed against by the same kind of injustice or wrongdoing. Perhaps Allison Jean realized her actions would not only affect Amber Guyger but others as well. By extending and embracing forgiveness, we can also insist on justice due to our role as "agents of redemptive disruption." This is why forgiveness should be the immediate decision to lament responsibly, process slowly, and release our right to retaliate, in order to heal, reconcile, and disrupt systems that are purveyors of injustice and violence. The immediate decision to forgive anchors the act of forgiveness in faith in Christ, even as we realize the impossibility of forgiving without the aid of the Holy Spirit. Forgiveness is a process that includes lament, mental processing, and a decision to "let go and let God."

Forgiveness is giving and getting life back afresh after an egregious offense. In the words of Jackson, "To fore-give is not to wipe away all memory of sin—that would be irresponsible—but it is to fore-get, to get one's life back in advance of anything another might do or not do."[29] In this way, Christians who forgive are participants in the effects of Christ's resurrection. To live in Christ is to experience life in, through, and after the pain and suffering caused by the offenses of others. Because of the cross at Calvary, we are forgiven; thus, we are expected to forgive as an infectious sign of God's grace to us.

Forgiveness: The Hope of Redemption

There must be more to forgiveness than the assuagement of guilt or an elixir of emotional pain, where everyone goes on their merry way after forgiveness is extended. Rutledge rightly attests that "forgiveness by itself . . . does not satisfy the human craving for justice; more important still, it does not fully express either the power or the love of God."[30] Forgiveness is a testament to the power of the love of God and its ultimate triumph over evil. Forgiveness resides in the eternal promise of redemption that God, through Christ, will make all things new. No matter the pain, "our light affliction, which is but for a moment, worketh for us a far more exceeding and eternal weight of glory" (2 Cor 4:17 KJV).

Forgiveness is a cataclysmic and transformative action that reverberates into the future. Jackson states, "Forgiveness is an 'eternal' work."[31]

Forgiveness, more than anything else, is the pronouncement that evil and injustice are temporal realities, limited in their time and impact because of the incalculable and incomprehensible love of God. Evils such as slavery, Jim Crow, systemic injustice, police brutality, redlining, and unjust criminal judicial systems seek to conquer and control God's agenda for kingdom unity. Forgiveness is just one action of disruption that prevents evil from taking root and sprouting wherever it is sown. Forgiveness is the constant reminder that love and mercy are greater powers that prevent evil from multiplying by blocking the growth of the seeds of bitterness in the hearts of the injured.

Forgiveness seeks truth. Though confessions may never come, and change may be slow, forgiveness shouts "this is wrong" from the rooftops. Forgiveness does not turn a blind eye to injustice. It is tough love that calls out the dastardly deeds perpetrated and forced upon poor communities when police brutality, voter disenfranchisement, economic exploitation, environmental pollution, and limited health options are the order of the day. Forgiveness is a rebuttal when injustice attempts to cloak itself in normative activity. Of forgiveness, James Harris states, "Its power lies in the ability to make things new. To interpret in a brand-new way this thing that has caused so much agony."[32]

The cross represents the most profound symbol of redemption and freedom known to humanity. At the cross, both natural and spiritual forces are at work attempting to rob onlookers and future believers of total freedom. All the authority of injustice, death, and spiritual bondage are overcome by Jesus's acts of redemption on the cross. These acts of redemption include extending forgiveness. Although some would argue that the acts committed by Amber Guyger and Dylann Roof are justifiably unforgivable, the words of Martin Luther King Jr. ring true: "As you press on for justice, be sure to move with dignity and discipline, using only the weapon of love. Let no man pull you so low as to hate him."[33]

Knowing the God of Justice

The God of the Bible is a God of justice. Biblical theology shows justice as a major attribute of the Triune God. "But the Lord of hosts is exalted in justice, and the Holy God shows himself holy in righteousness" (Isa 5:16). John N. Oswalt's commentary on Isaiah 5:16 is clear: "This verse is of great theological importance, for it expresses the truth of what makes God truly God; what sets him off as divine is neither his overwhelming power nor his mysterious numinousness. Rather, what marks him as God is his essential justice and righteousness."[34]

The justice of God is a derivative of God's steadfast love (*hesed*), which is a constant Old Testament characteristic of God's special covenantal love for God's people (Exod 34.6–7; Lam 3:22–23; Jer 9:24; Ps 136:6–9). Bruce C. Birch shows the relationship between God's steadfast love and God's justice: "God's holiness and God's steadfast love are expressed in their particular dimensions by a wide variety of biblical terms descriptive of the nature and work of God, especially in the covenant relationship to Israel. Perhaps the most important of these for the concerns of Christian ethics are God's righteousness (*sedeq*, masc.; *sedaqah*, fem.) and God's justice (*mispat*)."[35]

God *calls* for justice as the chief advocate of the oppressed, dispossessed, and marginalized because "almost as a corollary to God's partiality to the dispossessed is God's implacable opposition to evil in the world—all those forces that make for dispossession: injustice, oppression, economic exploitation, personal greed, and manipulation of others."[36] The prophets also attest to the justice of God: "Render true judgments, show kindness and mercy to one another, do not oppress the widow, the fatherless, the sojourner, or the poor, and let none of you devise evil against another in your heart" (Zech 7:9–10). Yahweh's call for justice is inherent in the Torah, the Prophets, and the Writings.

Steadfast love and justice are eternal attributes of God's person, but because of sin they are lost and fleeting realities in God's creation. Justice is necessary because evil is a reality within God's creation. Genesis 3 records the fall of humanity and the introduction of evil and sin into the world by Satan. Likewise, the *protoevangelium* in Genesis 3 incorporates God's immediate and decisive response to the problem of evil and sin by declaring that through the promised seed of the woman, Satan, the very source of evil and sin, will be crushed, thereby ultimately eradicating all of evil's attendant offspring, among which is *injustice*.

Prayer and Justice

The parable of the persistent widow in Luke 18 exposes the reader to poignant insights into one of the most effective practices of social justice activism and its results: prayer and collective vindication. Darrell Bock provides theological insight into prayer and the vindication of God as it relates to Luke 18: "The need for their rescues is expressed in their constant entreating God. Luke elsewhere uses Βοάω (boaō) to describe the cry of those in need of mercy (9:38; 18:38), and the sense is the same here. Believers are under pressure, so they are to pray as the passage exhorts them to do. God is listening."[37] God hears cries for justice.

With faithful, collective prayer unto God, the oppressed people of God believed in a God who would vindicate them because of their cries. This parable proves a vital aspect of the activist's methods in social justice activism: "If you are suffering some kind of injustice, the right strategies and constant prayer can actually persuade the powerful to grant you justice."[38] The oppressed activists believed that as Christians, they were indeed the elect of God. They believed that they could "take it to the Lord in prayer."

Prayer is the foundation of African American spirituality and the bedrock of social justice activism. Prayer ties activists to the purposes of God through social justice activism and supplies them with a perpetual fount of comfort, guidance, and spiritual vitality through perpetual communion with God. Prayer gives the activists courage, resilience, and determination. The African American scholar, pastor, and mystic Howard Thurman explains,

> Prayer grows out of an imperative urgency, sometimes pointed, sometimes diffused. It enables one to keep fresh and focused in spirit the

dedication to which one's life is given. Again and again, it creates a profound sense of power deep within the mind, expressing itself in strange new courage and purposefulness. The first manifestation of this courage is the attack that it makes on the basis of one's external fears of people and circumstance. Prayer often yields a buoyancy and joyousness of spirit as the overtone of a relaxed confidence in God. . . . Without this, nothing quite has meaning; with this, all the rest of the journey, however difficult, however painful, however devastating, will be filled with a music all its own.[39]

Dallas Willard believes every believer can have perpetual communion with God. This sustained prayer life involves "speaking and being spoken to."[40] The mass prayer rallies in the civil rights movement are a perfect example of this kind of perpetual communion, since activists always needed new refreshment, new strategies, and clearer direction. The "prayer rallies" that were held in African American churches on specific evenings during the week in various cities throughout the United States during the mid-1960s were times of planning protest methods and sharing information while also being times of spiritual formation. In the prayer rallies, individual pray-ers lead the masses in prayers requesting God's intervention in their righteous cause for freedom, justice, and love. In these meetings, the marchers, protesters, and activists gained a renewed strength for their weary souls and tired feet. The prayers gave new life and sustained hope to those who felt that justice was a delayed or denied reality. Through prayer, the activist's heart was kept pure and free of the temptations of hatred and revenge, lest any "'root of bitterness' springs up and causes trouble" (Heb 12:15).

Dietrich Bonhoeffer witnessed the fervor of these powerful prayer rallies in New York while serving as a Sunday school teacher in the all-Black Abyssinian Baptist Church, led by the revered Adam Clayton Powell Sr. Bonhoeffer's time in Harlem and at Abyssinian was so impactful that "some of the ideas and language Powell used in preaching came up in Bonhoeffer's own literary work. Most of all, Bonhoeffer's experience in Harlem and in this church informed his witness in Nazi Germany."[41] The prayerful activity in such gatherings resembled what Dietrich Bonhoeffer describes as "The Day Together," a time of communal spiritual formation. Bonhoeffer writes, "Often in the Christian community there will be a desire for special prayer fellowship beyond the daily prayers of common devotions. . . . Such meetings should be held only where there is a common desire for them and where it is certain that there will be common participation in definite hours of prayer."[42] In these rallies, everyone was aware of the power and necessity of prayer and was committed to active participation.

For these activists, praying was not a means to manipulate God, for they knew the results were of the power of God and not their human exploits. As they prayed and believed, the activists recognized that any legislative or social victory was a result of God's mercy and grace. Charles T. Collins Winn describes the motives and mindset of these prayers: "Our prayers and longing for God to act is both passive and active. It is a spiritual practice that grounds us in the fact that only God can truly create a new reality in our world. We must continually receive it as a gift of God, for it is not in our power to create a new world."[43] Even amid disappointing news, activists continued to believe in the power of prayer. Many prayers resembled the prayers of the people of Israel: "O Lord, how long shall I cry for help, and you will not hear? Or cry to you 'Violence!' and you will not save? Why do you make me see iniquity, and why do you idly look at wrong? Destruction and violence are before me; strife and contention arise. So the law is paralyzed, and justice never goes forth. For the wicked surround the righteous; so justice goes forth perverted" (Hab 1:2–4).

Praying in the Spirit sustains the Christian social activists amid the threats of otherwise unconquerable darkness. John Wimber argues, "Evil powers, authorities and institutions are committed to spreading injustice, oppression, hatred, bigotry, cruelty, tyranny, brutality and anything else that stands against the kingdom of God."[44] Dr. Martin Luther King Jr. spoke of the Spirit's working in this manner in his sermon "Why Jesus Called a Man a Fool":

And immediately the telephone started ringing and I picked it up. On the other end was an ugly voice. . . . I'd heard these things before but for some reason that night it got to me. I turned over and I tried to sleep but I couldn't sleep. I was frustrated, bewildered. And then I got up and went back to the kitchen and I started warming some coffee, thinking that coffee would give me a little relief. . . . I pulled back on the theology and philosophy that I had just studied in the universities, trying to give philosophical and theological reasons for the existence and the reality of sin and evil, but the answer didn't quite come there. Something said to me, you can't call on Daddy now; he's up in Atlanta a hundred and seventy-five miles away. You can't call on Mama now. You've got to call on that something in the person that your daddy used to tell you about. . . . And I discovered then that religion had to become real to me and I had to know God for myself. And I bowed down over that cup of coffee—I never will forget it. And . . . I prayed a prayer and I prayed out loud that night. . . . I said, "Lord, I'm down here trying to do what's right. . . . But Lord, I must confess that I'm weak now; I'm faltering; I'm losing my courage. . . ." And it seems at that moment that I could hear an inner voice saying to me, Martin Luther, stand up for righteousness.[45]

Preaching and Justice

It is a common refrain among African American preachers that "preaching and prayer go together." Preaching as a spiritual discipline is the result of the divine activity taking place between God and the called preacher. In the case of social justice activism, the African American preacher believes the role of prophetic preaching is one with the Old Testament prophets. Historically, those who spoke the word of the Lord from African American pulpits spoke to individuals and institutions about social injustices that attempted to restrict the plan of God for ethnic minorities. That kind of preaching is referred to as prophetic preaching—speaking truth to power. Moses is the model prophet for the African American preacher. Luke Timothy Johnson comments, "Moses is the perfect prototype of the prophet. Moses 'knew' the Lord face to face; he heard all the words that the Lord wanted the people to hear."[46] Moses was sent by God and, through communion with God, received instruction to confront the injustices perpetrated upon the people of God by Pharaoh and his empire. In this manner, preaching is a spiritual act of obedience. The spiritual act of social justice preaching bore resemblance to the prophetic ministry of the Old Testament. Johnson also argues that "the prophet is not only empowered by God; the prophet speaks for God. . . . The human word spoken by the prophet can be called 'God's word' because they communicate to other humans God's perspective on the human situation they share, communicating as well, God's vision for humanity that the present circumstances impede."[47]

When the African American preacher activists were threatened to "tone down" sermons that centered on social justice activism, obedience to the call of God fueled their commitment to prophetic preaching and speaking truth to power. This practice is not unique to African American spiritual expressions, since "the Old Testament prophets have long since been seen as quasi-models for Christian social crisis preaching, for they were ever relating social and political well-being to religion in their preaching."[48] Paul House likewise speaks to the spiritual obedience of the prophet when he contends that "[the prophet] Amos particularly focuses on the theme of justice. The prophets decry oppression of all kinds, including that created by false oaths . . . and dishonest scales."[49] Preaching as a spiritual discipline within the African American prophetic preaching tradition is described this way by the distinguished African American scholar Robert Franklin: "I provide an interpretation of black church culture and its core traits and note that prophetic preaching is rooted in, and emanates from, a rich congregational culture with the following features: emotionally expressive, sensory engaging worship; cathartic shouting; triumphal song; therapeutic congregational prayer; and politically empowering religious education."[50]

Social concern and prophetic zeal are unique aspects of African American preaching. From the Reconstruction Era after the Civil War to the present, Black preachers and Black preaching have liberated the Black masses from the torture and terror of injustice. Henry Mitchell writes, "Black preaching of the Reconstruction Era could be considered a tremendous success when it simply enabled Blacks to survive massive brutality and injustice. . . . Black preachers more than any other single group were able to mobilize the saints who marched and marched in the sixties, until the walls came tumbling down."[51]

The plight of Black people coupled with the unique ability of the Black preacher to interpret and apply the biblical narrative of God's involvement in the liberation of God's people allowed both preacher and people to see a God who was involved in their struggle for freedom, just as God was for the Israelite people. Cleophus J. LaRue states, "A God who is unquestionably for them is what blacks see when they go to Scriptures. Thus, the distinctive power of black preaching is to be found, first and foremost, in that which blacks believe Scripture reveals about the sovereign God's involvement in the everyday affairs and circumstances of their marginalized existence."[52] In this sense, preaching is also communal. Walter Brueggemann testifies, saying, "Prophetic preaching can take place only where the preacher is deeply embedded in the YHWH narrative. When the listening community is also embedded in there or at least has a residual attachment to that narrative, a change for engagement is offered."[53]

Practice of Community

The practice of community was another spiritually forming discipline that aided activists in their stand for social justice. Among socially oppressed people, both the educated and uneducated suffer the same injustices; a Black family fortunate enough to have bank accounts and college degrees has experienced the same closed doors as the uneducated, poor single mother living in the ghetto. Suffering social restriction and social dislocation in almost every venue of life was and is the reality of the dispossessed.

Social activists practiced the simplicity of communal living to show charity while they worked for justice. Twentieth-century activists knew that extending charity and working for justice were needed in the work of social justice. Charity was needed to *alleviate* the sufferings caused by injustice, while working toward justice was needed to *eliminate* the injustices that caused the sufferings: "Charity comes from those with plenty who chose to dole out their excess to the poor. Justice comes from those of all walks of life who seek to bring about lasting and long-term change in the distribution of resources."[54] In the African American church, sharing and giving with "the least of these" became a spiritual practice that was necessary for community cohesiveness. This spiritual principle is a work of the Spirit enacted upon the first-century church. In the book of Acts, a marginalized people met the needs of one another by living in community as they "had all things in common. And they were selling their possessions and belongings and distributing the proceeds to all, as any had need" (Acts 2:44–45). Much like that community, the African American community experienced this same "holy communalism, this sacred sociality,"[55] which was an expression of divine love.

The sin of greed in the world causes economic injustice. Injustices are almost always economically motivated. Often it is the greed of a few that causes need among many. Cappadocian Church Father Saint Basil the Great speaks to this in his homily:

> Who are the greedy? Those who are not satisfied with what suffices for their own needs. Who are the robbers? Those who take for themselves what rightfully belongs to everyone. And you, are you not greedy? Are you not a robber? The things you received in trust as a stewardship, have you not appropriated them for yourself? Is not the person who strips another of clothing called a thief? And those who do not clothe the naked when they have the power to do so, should they not be called the same? The bread you are holding back is for the hungry, the clothes you keep put away are for the naked, this shows they are rotting away with disuse are for those who have none, the silver you

keep buried in the earth is for the needy. You are thus guilty of injustice toward as many as you might have aided, and did not.[56]

Reconciliation Is the Goal of Activism

Love of neighbor is the motive for reconciliation and the spirit that sustains activism. Social justice activism begins not with seeking civil rights or even the righting of injustices but with the love of neighbor. If activism seeks economic, civil, or social rights while taking no interest in the one who withholds these rights, this is not Christian social justice activism. The end of Christian social justice activism is never aimed at the mere obtaining of rights or privileges. African American social justice activists of the twentieth century were filled with love even for their oppressors. What has distinguished Christian social justice activists from political pundits and charlatans masquerading as people of good will is their willingness to see the oppressors as children of God. To view them as *imago Dei* despite their hate-filled spirit, through the eyes of love. Kierkegaard defines this love ethic and commands us to "love those we see . . . loving is loving the very person one sees. The emphasis is not on loving the perfections one sees in a person, but on loving the person one sees, whether or not one sees perfections or imperfection in this person."[57] An African American spirituality sought egalitarianism within institutions through a moral-ethical mandate to love.

Love motivated Martin Luther King Jr.'s vision of the "beloved community." In King's thinking, "Love does this by insisting that justice be done in human relationships, because justice cannot be separated from love. Indeed, justice is not the antithesis of love but constitutes its inner meaning."[58] God created us to live in community and harmony with one another. One can obtain civil rights and remain outside the design of God's plan for humanity. When activism is motivated by love and a realized, biblically informed eschatological vision, where people from every nation, from all tribes and peoples and languages, can live in communion with one another, reconciliation is a viable possibility. This spirituality, which is biblical, communal, and motivated in love, creates a commonality among people that will lead to the dismantling of the lies of racial and ethical superiority, root causes of injustice. Matthew Lamb explains, "A Christian spirituality . . . goes to the root of the evil haunting history in its refusal to make any compromises with dominative power. It takes us just as we are, wherever we are, and beckons us to attend more intelligently and responsibly to who we are and what we are. If we so attend to who we are we shall gradually discover that we as human persons are intrinsically related to all other human persons who ever have, are, or will live on the face of this earth."[59]

The creation of this community called for twentieth-century social justice activists to demand that those in power reform the institutions that provided them security and to abandon a lifestyle that perpetuated cultural dislocation of the other. Hanigan states, "To achieve reconciliation and to reveal truth . . . a person must first of all take an active stand against the structures, systems, and social injustices that hide the truth and make reconciliation impossible."[60] The love that creates the new community where injustice is unwelcome will come with great sacrifices if it is to be realized. This is not a fuzzy, emotion-filled, utopian type of love, where the oppressed and the oppressor simply "just get along" and "pray about it." No, this love calls for sacrifices of comfort and conveniences, of friends and family, of reputations and respectability. Luther Ivory speaks of the ministerial and personal sacrifices of creating the beloved community:

> The fundamental question is whether or not we are prepared to pay the cost of orienting our personal lifestyles that is required of a co-participating agent in God's restoration of the human community. . . . King admitted that this lifestyle requires moving beyond token gestures and individual acts of moralistic philanthropy based on notions of pity. Personal, sacrificial suffering through the dogged emancipatory praxis of nonviolent civil resistance becomes both a moral and political necessity. This meant some might suffer the loss of home, family, property, power, prestige, security and possibly

life itself. King's perspective continues to ask whether or not any of us are ready, willing, and able to pay the price to achieve the justice we claim we desire.[61]

African American Christian spirituality included agape love. Those who participated in the sacred work of social activism embodied agape love for the sake of creating a reconciled, new community where love and justice are inherent qualities. The spirituality of twentieth-century social justice activists provides a blueprint for the unending work of social justice activism in the twenty-first century. The activists of the twentieth century understood that the Bible presents, from its opening pages, a God of justice and love. The activists who intentionally engaged in private and communal prayer were empowered to display the courage to face the nightmarish environments where injustice flourished. Prophetic preaching was birthed out of prayer and experienced in the context of community, where needs were met through loving channels of mercy and charity. Perhaps the greatest lesson that Christians of every race and ethnicity can learn from twentieth-century African American Christian social justice activists is to seek the will of God through the ministry of reconciliation (2 Cor 5:18). It is only in this spirit that an eschaton of hope will replace the spirit of despair in a world groaning for justice.

Sacred Self-Care

Rest for the Weary Radical

PROPHETIC RADICALISM AS Christian proclamation *and* living *exposes* the root causes of injustice and *advocates* for God's redemptive justice while *acting* in accord with the life and ministry of Christ through the power of the Holy Spirit. Pastors who engage in this sacred labor enter a daring and daunting work that makes demands upon the whole person. The year 2020 will be remembered as a year of formidable challenge and painful social conflict for America, where prophetic radicalism was required. That year, I had the privilege to carry the burden of addressing these social crises through countless speaking or preaching engagements and participating in no less than five peaceful protest marches or demonstrations and seven panel discussions. One of those panel discussions, hosted by the Houston Metropolitan Baptist Minister's Conference, was entitled "Two Pandemics: Social Injustice and COVID-19," precisely describing the aura and milieu of that deadly year.

The Covid-19 pandemic hit the world with a force unseen since the 2009 Swine Flu pandemic. On March 13, 2020, President Donald Trump declared Covid-19 a public health emergency by issuing two national emergency declarations under the Stafford Act and the National Emergency Act.[1] Within days, both state and municipal governments followed suit by issuing stay-at-home orders designed to stop the rapid spread of the deadly virus. Amid the fear and frustration of the pandemic, social and racial unrest sparked national demonstrations, protests, and riots in response to several fatal encounters between unarmed African Americans and law enforcement. Among those were the killings of Breonna Taylor, George Floyd, and Daunte Wright.

On March 13, 2020, twenty-six-year-old Louisville, Kentucky, emergency response worker Breonna Taylor was shot multiple times and killed inside her home by Louisville Metro Police officers. Perhaps the most egregious police crime in recent memory occurred on May 25, 2020, when Minneapolis Police officer Derek Chauvin kneeled on the neck of George Floyd for nine and a half minutes, killing him during an arrest where Floyd was alleged to have presented a storekeeper with a fake twenty-dollar bill. Months later, in a suburb of Minneapolis and while the trial of Chauvin was taking place, twenty-year-old Daunte Wright was shot during a routine traffic stop. There were others. In fact, Al Jazeera reported that in the year after Floyd's murder, police across the United States killed 1,068 people.[2] This is not to suggest that all these deaths involving police since the Floyd murder were unjustified or that excessive use of force was used. However, such news is soul-crushing and brings inexorable weariness to those who are justifiably skeptical of encounters between law enforcement and poor people of color, which make up an overwhelming majority of those cases.[3]

There are few American Christians who can testify that they were not affected by the events of 2020. The pandemic left many jobless, and once-flourishing businesses shut down due to federal, state, and local mandates to shelter in place. Although there were efforts from Congress to stimulate the economy through stimulus checks, the qualifying stipulations still rendered many ineligible. The reporting of mental health concerns reached new highs as domestic violence, child abuse, and suicide cases became painfully visible reminders of how a pandemic could expose the horrors that lie beneath the surface of neglected, powerless, and impoverished communities. This barrage of spiritual and social concerns became a threat to my own mental and physical health. Weariness renders a silent but powerful assault upon the soul and body of those who labor to see the world right.

The Cause of Weariness: Knowing and Responsibility

Weariness comes in many forms for radical disciples who dare act as disrupters and disturbers of the status quo. Identifying the root causes of this weariness is essential for pastors who are seeking to center, revitalize, and practice self-care. Weariness can feel like darkness, drought, and a period of deep silence where it seems as if God is absent. The esteemed pastor, theologian, and mystic Howard Thurman speaks to the importance of identifying the source or cause of our weariness: "There comes a time of dryness in life; everything seems to be at low tide. There is no sharp, tragic moment; no great or sudden draining of one's powers—only the silent loss of enthusiasm for living. Nothing seems to matter—just a great dryness of the spirit. . . . The time of drought may be seasonal, or it may be specially circumstanced. It is therefore of greatest importance to understand its cause, and to discover early in life what special reserves must be tapped to bring flowing fully and freshly the refreshing, life-giving currents."[4]

THE BURDEN OF KNOWING

Knowing produces a unique burden. This statement is complimentary to the timeworn phrase "ignorance is bliss," which suggests that the less we know, the happier we are and, potentially, the easier the state of living becomes. But weariness is often directly related to the painful knowledge that the world is not as it ought to be. It also stems from the deeper awareness of *why* things are not how they ought to be and the yearning desire to see them as they should be. The image that comes to mind comes from Luke 19:41–42, as Jesus weeps over Israel. His weariness and weeping are the result of his knowing and discerning what others could not. He says, "Would that you, even you, had known on this day the things that make for peace! But they are hidden from your eyes" (Luke 19:42). The pastor who has been granted insight into the conditions of the world and into the hearts of people will also carry a heavy burden, one that many will fail to understand or see. Jesus's weeping provides a picture of the prophetic burden of knowing.

Many of us have trusted that the world could be just if we were willing to put in the hard work of making it so and if we believed in ourselves and gave people the benefit of the doubt. But it's not that simple. Some naïvely believe that everyone who attends church and professes to be Christian desires all communities to flourish and that America is the noblest of all nations, a Christian nation that all can call home, or racism doesn't exist because, like in professional sports, "we are all on the same team." When one comes to the realization that those statements deserve critical reflection and examination, the burden of that realization is a palpable reality.

As children, my brother and I had a favorite TV show called *The Dukes of Hazzard*. The show starred cousins Bo and Luke Duke, who were on probation in rural Hazzard County, Georgia. The highlight of every episode was the way the cousins managed to elude, outrun, and escape Sheriff Rosco P. Coltrane in their orange 1969 Dodge Charger, which they affectionately called "General Lee." General Lee had a Confederate flag prominently painted on its roof, which was unavoidably and proudly displayed every show. The fact that Bo and Luke Duke were always portrayed as moral, upstanding citizens, even though they were convicts, was overlooked because they often foiled illegal activity in Hazzard County and constantly blocked the governmental corruption of greedy County Commissioner Jefferson Davis (J. D.) "Boss" Hogg.

As a child, I never questioned the anti-American and racist symbolism of the show—the Confederate flag adorning the brothers' beloved car (cherished almost as much as the human characters), which was named for the notorious slaveholding general of the Confederacy, Robert E. Lee, and one of the other main characters named after the President of the Confederacy, Jefferson Davis, a slaveholder and proslavery advocate. I was innocent, blind, and oblivious to the anti-Black symbolism paraded for my amusement every week. My failure to connect the dots between the characters and their real-life heroes perpetuated the myths that anti-Blackness was harmless as long as it was cloaked in a fast muscle car "straightening the curves, flattening the hills."[5] The year 2020 was also a year when the hotly contested arguments over Confederate statues took center stage. A retrospective look at *The Dukes of Hazzard* through the lens of 2020's arguments about the Confederacy's legacy made me wonder how I would have felt back in the late '70s and early '80s if I had realized what those symbols stood for.

Prophetic radicalism involves knowing that produces a unique burden. Burdens cause weariness. In prophetic radicalism, the burden is often one that is made heavy when pastors and congregations discover truth from beneath the veneer and veil that often cover injustice from the eyes of the trusting. When motives are revealed, plans are uncovered, lies are discovered, and trusted authorities are forced to show their hand, the cumulative effect of this social justice work is deep weariness. When the government orders the shutdown of DMV offices or voter registration in rural Black communities, the long, often futile work of protesting on grounds of racial disenfranchisement results in weariness.[6] When the community is apprised that the latest census results require redistricting to increase minority-majority voting districts but the majority is resistant and noncompliant, this too increases the weariness of those who believed that when people "know better, they will do better."

THE BURDEN OF RESPONSIBILITY

Knowing and responsibility are inseparable. Awareness should birth action. When we become aware of injustices, we cannot ignore the call to engage the causes. A moral person cannot "know" and fail to act. However, embracing moral and ethical responsibility can also produce a weariness that can potentially subvert the work of prophetic radicalism. Accepting responsibility brings its own burdens and can lead to weariness caused by the inevitable confrontation of powers and forces that have unlimited resources and that also have the propensity to do violence.[7] Second, weariness of responsibility can derive from the dual factors of adopting a messiah complex and the failure to create a community of collaboration. Without an intentional plan aimed at restoring and refreshing the soul, the radical pastor can become tired, embattled, and beset by bitterness.

Confronting the Powers That Be

In his award-winning book *The Powers That Be: Theology for a New Millennium*, Walter Wink contends, "When the powers that be catch the merest whiff of God's new order, they automatically mobilize all their might to crush it."[8] Exposing, advocating, and acting for the cause of justice can be wearing and wearying because of the constant requirement of having to confront and deal with powerful people in order to see the dawn of justice. Powerful people never relinquish power voluntarily. In this shadowy reality, violence can and will be employed when diplomacy fails to quiet and still the efforts of those who seek to resist their program. The threat of violence is always present. Anyone who has ever engaged in justice work can feel its breath on the neck and can sense its shadow lurking in the background where the powerful look for any justification to unleash it. Throughout the course of my ministry as a pastor and as the president of the Tuscaloosa chapter of the Southern Christian Leadership Conference, I learned the weariness of facing powerful entities and the frustration of having to navigate complex laws, policies, ordinances, and organizational structures just to get a hearing, not to mention the effort of making progress on an issue that seems unjust. The temptation to "just let it be" or to live with the dissatisfaction imposed upon a person or a community can be deflating and disheartening. And the accompanying fear of violence is always present.

When state and municipal governments exercise eminent domain, they can bring the full weight of their resources to oppose or threaten against any church, activist group, or individual that seeks to halt the transfer of property and wealth from those who have held it for generations to those with plans to gentrify for the sake of the "common good." Nowhere is this threat of weariness experienced more than in our criminal justice system. Poor and minority communities seldom approach judge and jury with the confidence of having their day in court. These families always feel, to borrow the words of Howard Thurman, that "their backs are constantly against the wall" in these spaces. The data confirms their suspicions. Alex Van Brunt reports that "95% of criminal cases end in plea bargaining. Excessive case-loads contribute to this treadmill, and result in a 'meet 'em and plead 'em' system of justice, in which clients have little more than a brief conversation in the courtroom with a harried public defender before pleading guilty."[9] The majority of poor offenders cannot afford a private attorney, so they have to rely on unprepared public defenders who often force them to take plea deals or suffer the consequences of the maximum sentence. It stands to reason that those who minister to communities of color experience this weariness with the criminal justice system as well.

According to the Equal Justice Initiative, "Black men are nearly six times more likely to be incarcerated than white men; Latino men are nearly three times likely. Native Americans are incarcerated at more than twice the rate of white Americas. The Bureau of Justice Statistics projected in 2001 that one of every three Black boys and one of six Latino boys born that year would go to jail or prison if trends continue."[10] With these haunting statistics, hope seems to be a fleeting reality, and weariness invites a punishing hopelessness that poor and minority communities often fail to escape.

In many cases, confronting injustice is really about convincing the powers that be to leverage their resources for the good of poor or neglected communities. Great labor and effort are required to convince mayors, city councilpersons, governors, state legislators, county commissioners, private businesses, and nonprofit organizations to come together to address poverty by sharing wealth and resources with underprivileged communities. This work can be daunting and exhausting. In many cases, the work of prophetic radicalism requires collecting mounds of data, securing enough votes to gain approval, and recruiting allies to help gain leverage to move the needle forward on *any* effort to help the poor in an impactful and sustaining way. This is work that requires the sacrifice of time and emotional energy.

The Messiah Complex: Weary Saviors

Martin Luther King Jr. accepted the call to become the pastor of Dexter Avenue Baptist Church in Montgomery, Alabama, on May 2, 1954. He was also immediately thrust into the position of president of the Montgomery Improvement Association at a meeting at Mt. Zion AME Church on December 5, 1955. From that day until his last, April 4, 1968, although there were many talented and eloquent people of conviction, Martin Luther King Jr. was the face of the civil rights movement. Many wanted to put King on a pedestal as a kind of messiah, as the most visible and important person in the movement. This anointing was understandable and noble, but some pointed to the movement's spirit of patriarchy that locked women out of leadership roles as less than noble. King's responsibilities took a toll on his health, family, and soul. Joseph Rosenbloom captures the weariness King experienced in the days leading up to the fateful day at the Loraine Hotel in Memphis, Tennessee: "Anyone who remembered him as a young man first embracing the civil rights cause in the mid-1950s would have been shocked by the change in his appearance. . . . There was something about him then, the freshness of the face and the limpid softness of his eyes that conveyed a boyish innocence. . . . Now, in 1968, he was a man in distress. His years in the movement had tested the limits of his courage and endurance. The strain had taken its toll emotionally and physically. He looked run-down, his eyes weary, face puffy, and neck straining against a white shirt collar."[11] These words describe how the fight for justice can wear on a person, especially when, by fault or default, they go at it alone.

The burden of responsibility becomes weariness when the pastor tries to go it alone to face adversaries who have unlimited resources and the propensity to do violence. African American pastors have been notorious for embodying a "messiah complex," taking on the obligation and expectation of being the sole savior of a people. Pastors often have led the fight for justice, in most cases standing alone. In the past, African American pastors were either the only or the most literate people in the African

American community, making them the default leaders and spokespeople for the community. A historical necessity grew into an impossible, unrealistic, and unnecessary expectation. The fact that pastors depended on their churches alone for financial support and were not employees of white establishments allowed them the freedom to speak out and represent their communities without fear of losing employment as a form of retribution.

The messiah complex in the Black church also stems from the sacred honor bestowed on the pastoral office by Black congregations. Historically, in Black Baptist churches, primarily due to the autonomy of the Baptist denomination, pastors have enjoyed free rein and have possessed complete authority over congregational matters. Most decisions, from the simplest to the most consequential, must meet the pastor's approval. Almost sacerdotal in concept, in Black churches, the office of pastor is still seen as a more exclusive, holy, and higher office than any other office in the church.

But this concept often comes with a high cost. The messiah complex may be thrust upon the pastor by the local congregation. But some pastors embrace and abuse this power, pursuing self-serving needs and seeking constant approval and adoration. Douglas Webster makes a compelling case when he says, "There are various stages of maturity and ability, but no spiritual elite. Not everyone is called to preach, but no one is more called than anyone else. We are all called to fulfill our calling."[12] When pastors are called upon to fight for justice out of a messiah complex, they can easily become easy targets for intimidation, ridicule, and slander. The demand to be present during council proceedings, the obligation to represent the community before the elite and powerful, and the expectations attached to attending to families who are victims of injustice add up. These and the weight of other expectations can wear down the lone-ranger pastor who embraces a messiah complex. Doing the work of justice is not a place for solo performances. It demands teamwork.

Restoring the Radical's Weary Soul

Identifying the factors that lead to weariness is one thing, but finding restoration and rest is another. Prophetic radicalism is hard work, and if the pastor is to engage in this type of justice work for the long haul, spiritual- and self-care must be priorities. Pastors who engage in prophetic radicalism and act as agents of disruption need to embrace spiritual disciplines such as detachment, radical togetherness, shared suffering, worship, and prayer. Those who engage in prophetic radicalism need these disciplines to restore their weary souls.

DETACHMENT

All the disciplines that will bring rest and restoration to the weary radical's soul are dependent on some form of detachment. But the practice of detachment in and of itself can prove to be futile, useless, and in some cases, dangerous if it is not accompanied by other life-giving nutrients of the Spirit. The discipline of detachment can help free the soul of clutter and noise. But detachment alone is not enough. Spiritual formation through detachment has a two-step spiritual purpose: to clean the soul of clutter and noise and to replenish it with the light and life of the Spirit. The two are interrelated and cannot exist without the other. Detachment requires attachment. Detachment helps to cleanse one's soul of the images, words, assaults, and other contaminants that are collected when one is engaged in prophetic radicalism. But restoring the soul also requires weary radicals to attach themselves to the word of God and the Holy Spirit to be in fellowship with God.

Mark 6 provides a stunning example of how those engaged in the grind and demands of prophetic radicalism need to detach from the burden and weariness of this heavy work to rest the body and soul. Jesus sends the twelve out to heal the sicknesses of the people and to preach the gospel of the kingdom (Mark 6:7–13). King Herod hears of this and thinks Jesus must be John the Baptist raised from the dead. Why? Because Herod had earlier ordered John to be beheaded because John *acted* as an agent of disruption.

John had *exposed* Herod's adulterous deeds and *advocated* for righteousness. The news about John and Herod's actions had no doubt reached the disciples. After many comings and goings of the disciples on their healing and preaching mission, Jesus decisively orders the apostles to "come away by yourselves to a desolate place and rest a while" (Mark 6:31). They were weary and needed to detach.

Because prophetic radicalism involves *exposing*, *advocating*, and *acting*, pastors and other disruptors will do well to detach from the physical, mental, and spiritual demands of justice work. Detachment is often necessary to avoid the depression that can come from the mental consumption of the constant barrage of images and news reports that often feature violence, poverty, and other forms of social ills and injustice. Detachment replaces death and darkness with life and light. Howard Thurman powerfully insists, "There is the rest of detachment and withdrawal when the spirit moves into depths of the region of the Great Silence, where world weariness is washed away and blurred vision is once again prepared for the focus of the long view where seeking and finding are so united that failure and frustration, real though they are, are no longer felt to be ultimately real."[13] I have made it a practice to avoid watching videos or musing over Facebook posts of police shootings, tasings, or brutal beatings of unarmed citizens. In equal measure, I refuse to watch video footage on social media of the senseless acts of violence perpetrated by Black youth in urban communities upon one another. Some of these videos are captured by people who are so desensitized to violence that they record people being beaten, stabbed, shot, and abused just for their sport and amusement.

All these traumatic images have the potential to do damage to the soul. The constant bombardment of videos with the caption "The following content could be upsetting or disturbing to some viewers" can sear pictures into the mind of the pastor whose Jeremiah-like sensitivity to humanity causes them to feel the pain of complete strangers in the video. These images cannot be easily erased. The footage of George Floyd pleading for his life, Eric Garner begging to breathe, Diamond Reynolds and her four-year-old daughter screaming in fear after Philando Castile was shot to death within inches of them, or the soul-wrenching dashcam and cell phone video of Texas state trooper Brian Encinia manhandling Sandra Bland can linger in the mind for weeks, if not forever. Detachment is necessary.

Detachment allows us to maintain not only our sanity but our humanity. Detachment from battling injustice keeps us from becoming embattled and bitter. Barbara L. Peacock wisely asserts, "Detachment from something or someone is the prerequisite for moving, living, and breathing in the directives God has planned and ordained for you."[14] When we detach, we acknowledge our humanity and our limitations in the perpetual quest for justice. But failure to detach signals pride and sometimes arrogance and a lack of trust in God, who ultimately gives us every victory in the fight for justice.

DETACHMENT AS A CONTINUOUS PRACTICE

Detachment is not a one-and-done practice. We must be intentional and proactive in meaningfully detaching from people, projects, and problems. Detachment could mean a weekend break to deactivate social media accounts, screen calls, watch a movie, read a book, or simply rest without leaving home. At other times, detachment could mean a semester or summer sabbatical. The thought here is that intentional and planned times of detachment set boundaries between the pastor and those in the pew. It also builds trust between the pastor and pew by emphasizing the shared accountability for pastoral responsibilities when the pastor is away. When detachment is practiced regularly, we include it in the normal rhythms of life, and we work and serve from a place of rest and not from a place of exhaustion and frustration.

Jesus employed the continuous practice of detachment in his ministry of prophetic radicalism. Detachment marks his ministry from its onset, when he was "led up by the Spirit into the wilderness" while "fasting forty days and forty nights" (Matt 4:1–2), to his final days of prayer in the Garden of Gethsemane. Barbara A. Holmes notes, "These rhythms of activism and contemplation, engagement and withdrawal resonate throughout his life."[15] It is also a practice he modeled and taught his disciples.

Mark 6:45 provides another example of Jesus insisting that the disciples "go before him to the other side" to pull away from the crowds due to the cost of discipleship. The noticeable dynamic in Mark 6 is the fact that Jesus calls the disciples to detach from what appears to be a very successful and impactful season of ministry because they "took up twelve baskets full of broken pieces and of the fish" (v. 43). This intense labor came after they assisted Jesus in feeding five thousand people. Pastors also can be driven by success, which often beckons for more success. Pastors can forget that effective and successful results are the direct results of God's power and grace and that it is not by *their* power or might but by the Spirit's. Our goal is to be faithful to the call and mission of God and to avoid using corporate criteria to measure success. Pastors can place enormous pressure on their shoulders to produce, when we are to be mindful that we are colaborers with God, who gives the increase to all that is accomplished through our efforts. Thus, the call to detach often requires detaching from "good" things.

Pastors should not underestimate the toll that effective ministry takes on the human mind and body. Even when it appears that our exposing, advocating, and acting are benefiting the masses and that the forces of evil are backpedaling, we must be intentional about detaching. No matter the highs or lows of our ministry, continuous moments of detachment are imperative. Thurman says it this way: "The need for periodic rest is not confined to mechanisms of various kinds. Rest may be complete inactivity when all customary functioning is suspended, and everything comes to a pause. Rest may be a variation in intensity, a contrast between loud and soft, high and low, strong and weak, a change of pace. Rest may be the complete shifting of scenery by the movement of objects or the person."[16]

Ministry in times of emergency and urgency presents the temptation to work until "the job is done," even if it causes exhaustion to set in. But the goal is not to work up to the point of exhaustion, of course. Taking continuous, planned, and disciplined seasons of detachment help the pastor avoid exhaustion.

Detaching during ministry's high points or in the middle of advocacy's most demanding season can be challenging because pastors desire to enjoy the fruits of victory, and they feel obligated to stay the course when times are challenging. Faithfulness to continuous seasons of detachment, regardless of the season of ministry, requires trust in the God of justice and reliance on a community committed to the practices of prophetic radicalism.

Radical Togetherness

Detachment does not mean disconnectedness. The weary radical pastor leans on community to find the rest the soul needs. Radical togetherness is an ecclesiological concept whereby the community of faith is conscious of the risks and rewards of prophetic radicalism and is willing to pursue justice by acting as a genuine community. Radical togetherness is the opposite practice of the messiah complex. "We are caught in an inescapable network of mutuality," Dr. Martin Luther King Jr. argued.[17] Jesus himself valued community with his twelve disciples, whom he taught, partnered with, suffered with, and called "friends." Not even Jesus, the Messiah, believed in the messiah complex as a model for ministry. He sent the disciples in pairs, commanded them to make other disciples, and after his ascension, empowered them as a community through the Holy Spirit.

Prophetic radicalism places the Christian in confrontation with the forces of evil, personified in powerful individuals responsible for sustaining the systems that wreak havoc on the poor and vulnerable. Because prophetic radicals are constantly being surrounded by enemies, Dietrich Bonhoeffer placed a premium on Christian community and therefore knew the necessity of intentional Christian community. In his classic book *Life Together*, he notes that, like Jesus, "the Christian, too, belongs not in the seclusion of a cloistered life but in the thick of foes. There is his commission, his work."[18] The New Testament constantly warns of the reality of living in a hostile world. This hostility makes prophetic radicalism necessary, and thus community is essential. Neither pastors nor pew are to live their lives avoiding and ignoring the manifestations of injustice; we are called to expose, advocate against, and prevent evils from becoming the norm by acting as agents of disruption. Pastors need a community to share the burdens of prophetic radicalism.

SHARED SUFFERING

Christians are admonished to "bear one another's burdens." Throughout the Christian Scriptures, shared suffering is a model for living in the church.[19] Moreover, the churches along the apostle Paul's missionary journeys and in his imprisonment share in his afflictions and suffering.[20]

In the infamous Bloody Sunday attack, state and local police bloodied John Lewis, Hosea Williams, and other civil rights demonstrators on the Edmund Pettus Bridge in Selma, Alabama. They were attempting to march to Montgomery, Alabama, following the murder of Jimmie Lee Jackson, who was fatally shot by police during a peaceful protest. But before Bloody Sunday, there was Bloody Tuesday in my hometown of Tuscaloosa, Alabama. Both days stand as examples of radical togetherness and shared suffering.

On Tuesday, June 9, 1964, Rev. T. Y. Rodgers, then pastor of the First African Baptist Church, assembled African American Christians from across Tuscaloosa and surrounding counties to protest segregated drinking fountains and restrooms in the county courthouse. According to then fifteen-year-old Danny Steele and his brother, CEO and President of the SCLC, Charles Steele, First African was often a gathering place for the congregations and Christians of Tuscaloosa to pray, plan demonstrations, and pass information concerning racial segregation in Tuscaloosa County. According to the Steele brothers, on June 9, 1964, although Rev. Rodgers and the leaders of the march knew that attack was imminent, they decided to march anyway. Steele adds, "Rev. Rodgers was committed to desegregate Tuscaloosa, and all of us were behind him 100%, and even though my parents warned me about going to the church on that day, I was determined to do my part even if it cost me getting in trouble."[21] According to Charles Steele, on Bloody Tuesday, local law enforcement and a violent, deputized mob threw tear gas through the windows of

First African Church, and when the peaceful worshippers inside ran out, the marchers beat them with bats, sticks, and bricks. Though Rev. Rodgers did not ask the people to risk their lives to disrupt a system of segregation, they were willing to suffer along with their leader.

The weary pastor is strengthened when the community is willing to share in the brunt of criticism, advocacy, and ostracism that often comes because of prophetic radicalism. We are called to rejoice with one another in victory but also to "weep with those who weep." In the body of Christ, "If one member suffers, all suffer together" (1 Cor 12:26).

CORPORATE WORSHIP

Prophetic radicalism becomes sacred activity only through worship. Prophetic radicalism is the sacred sacrifice that we submit to God as our worship. This worship sacrifice is what we present to God as people who are willing to give our very lives for God's glory. Activism can be a draining activity that depletes us of our spiritual energies and vitality. Just as enslaved Africans and disenfranchised African American Christians endured the abuses of white supremacy through being reminded of the hope and promises of God in song and prayers, so must the contemporary prophet and pew be refreshed through songs and prayers that lift up the faithfulness and ultimate victory of God in the face of evil and injustice.

When we are spiritually deprived, we easily drift into the dangerous waters of self-dependency, where prophetic radicalism becomes a joyless task that is engaged as meaningless obligation. Worship restores our souls. When prophetic radicalism ceases to have the glory of God as its foundational and primary objective, it becomes political activity up for grabs to the highest bidder. Richard Foster concurs: "If the Lord is to be *Lord*, worship must have priority in our lives. The *first* commandment of Jesus is, 'Love the Lord your God with all your heart, and with all your soul, and with all your mind, and all your strength' (Mark 12:30). The divine priority is worship first, service second. Our lives are to be punctuated with praise, thanksgiving, and adoration. Service flows out of worship. Service as a substitute for worship is idolatry. Activity is the enemy of adoration."[22]

Prophetic Radicalism as Sacred Work

A thin line exists between prophetic radicalism that glorifies God and self-aggrandizing showmanship. When pastors and pew are actively invested in bringing radical change to communities, newspapers and local and national TV news networks await a good headline. Social media platforms such as Instagram, Facebook, TikTok, and Twitter also serve as major outlets for the world to witness our activism. Avoiding media attention and steering clear of social media can be impossible, but guarding our motives and being intentional about who and what we promote are not.

When our activism becomes self-serving and fueled by people-pleasing actions, the spiritual potency required to make an impact soon wanes and slowly dies, and with it, we begin a slow death. Many activists start with noble intentions before losing focus due to the attention of media appearances, public speaking engagements, awards, and the allure of offerings of positions of power from organizations seeking talented, articulate, and courageous leaders. Attention-seeking and people-pleasing actions can become unforgiving taskmasters. The undisciplined soul can become intoxicated and addicted to media attention and overwhelmed by the constant demands of being "put on the program" every time a speaker or voice is needed. These actions lead to mental, physical, emotional, and spiritual weariness.

To avoid the slavery that comes from being driven by the agendas of the crowd and the impulses of our own fleshly desires, pastors must submit their lives and activism to God as worship. When our prophetic radicalism flows from a sincere place of worship, where we aim to give God glory, God's attention is the only attention that we will seek. Pastors who engage in prophetic radicalism must make "to him be the glory forever and ever" a daily declaration.

WORSHIP AND DEVOTION IN SONG

Worship also refreshes us when we are weary. Through worship, we cast our cares at the feet of Jesus, surrender our talents to his divine will, and acknowledge him as the ultimate source of righteousness and justice. As a boy, I remember the old saints singing, "Leave it there, leave it there, take your burden to the Lord and leave it there. If you trust and never doubt, he will surely bring you out. Take your burden to the Lord and leave it there."[23] The work of prophetic radicalism is what James Earl Massey describes as "a burdensome joy." However, it is a burden, nonetheless. Burdens worn and carried too long can cause weariness. The essential place to unload the burdens of human deprivation, social justice, violence, poverty, crime, and lack of joy is in worship. Here again, the Black church tradition aids people of every ethnic persuasion in its profound spirituality expressed through song.

Justice-loving people of many cultures have been touched and empowered by the African American spirituals and freedom songs. Howard Thurman goes on record to tell of a hymn request from Mahatma Gandhi when a group of African Americans visited him. The hymn "Were You There When They Crucified My Lord" is "the most universally beloved of all the hymns about Jesus." The lyrics are deeply moving: "Were you there when they crucified my Lord? Were you there when they crucified my Lord? Oh! Sometimes it causes me to tremble, tremble, tremble; Were you there when they crucified my Lord." Thurman states, "It cuts across differences of religion, race, class, and language, and dares to affirm that the key to the mystery of the cross is found deep within the heart of the experience itself."[24] Likewise, Dietrich Bonhoeffer, introduced to the Black spirituals during his time in Harlem and attendance at the Abyssinian Baptist Church in 1930, was deeply impacted and influenced by their melody and message. The German theologian, though not impressed with American seminaries, found solace in the worship experience at Abyssinian, and according to Reggie L. Williams, "the audience participation during the sermon and the black spirituals were all extremely moving for him." Bonhoeffer's close friend Eberhard Bethge admits that Bonhoeffer was so influenced by the spirituals that he collected recordings and later introduced his students to them. The distinctive nature of the songs that are sung in the Black church springs forth from the unique pain and indignities suffered by a people who still voice hope in the Sovereign God and who yet believe that "Jesus will fix it after 'while."

Worship is a lifestyle and should not be limited to a specific day or time or to the expressions of song, dance, prayer, communion, and preaching. Worship encompasses all those elements, and they are essential to restoring the soul of the weary radical. Corporate worship is life-giving and inspiring. In the presence of the saints, there is the potential for solace, consolation, and strength. In worship, the soul can be laid bare before God and be restored by God.

Diana L. Haynes reminds us of how generations of slaves who longed for freedom and justice articulated their hope not in literary material but rather through song. Weary radicals are to be reminded of how those before us were sustained through music and song. Haynes comments, "As an oral rather than literate people, it is understandable that the slaves, regardless of faith, did not describe their faith in God, Jesus, and the Holy Spirit in books or other written forms. Rather, it was preserved in their hearts and souls."[25] Known as "sorrow songs," these slave songs professed social and communal determination, theological identity, eschatological hope, and theological understanding. Moreover, these songs articulate weariness and burden. W. E. B. Du Bois correctly observes that these spirituals "are the music of an unhappy people, of the children of disappointment; they tell of death and suffering and unvoiced longing toward a truer world, of misty wanderings and hidden ways."[26] After emancipation, the quest for freedom did not cease; the toil and struggle for humanity and dignity continued in and by the Black church, who continued to sing their way to freedom in various genres of music. The sorrow songs gave way to hymns and later to gospel music. Hayes suggests, "Although they are still sung, they also gave birth to a more contemporary form of religious music, gospel music, which also comes from the heart of the Black community, providing Black people in modern times a place of quiet refuge as well as a stimulant for action."[27]

In every era of Black people's fight for justice, these songs professed social and communal determination, theological identity, eschatological hope, and theological understanding. The community in slavery dreamt of seeing justice one day, and from the cotton fields, they sang, "Freedom, Freedom, Freedom over me; And before I'll be a slave, I'll be buried in my grave and go home to my Lord and be free." Although sold as cattle, disinherited, and dehumanized, they sang the hymn of theological identity: "I know I am a child of God, although I move so slow. I'll wait until the vict'ry comes and move at God's command." Feeling hopeless through the long nights of inequality and the extended days of Jim Crow, the grand-sons and granddaughters of slaves sang, "I'm bound for Mount Zion, way out on the hill, I'm bound for Mount Zion way out on the hill; If anybody make it surely I will." Most importantly, the songs express a profound trust in God. Though forbidden and denied access to public education for much of our sojourn in America, the songs from the Black church, sometimes in folk dialect, possessed theological accuracy that is anchored in biblical literalism. The lyrics "My Lord delivered Daniel, my Lord deliv-ered Daniel, My Lord delivered Daniel. Why can't he deliver me?" insist that Daniel's escape from the lion's den and Nebuchadnezzar's grip was a victory owed to the Lord, who loves them as much as he loved Daniel.

Worship in song is an important discipline for the weary radical pas-tor. Worship in song, whether in private or with the corporate community, allows for unpacking cares and burdens in complete trust to our loving God. In song we also shower God with adoration and praise. Singing provides us with the experience of reconnecting with God for the life-giving grace our souls need. In song we are reminded of our finite being and our impotence, thus providing us an opportunity to be amazed in wonder and praise of God's power working in us. Singing reconnects us to beauty and fills us with hope. Worship in song refreshes and restores the soul of the weary radical.

WORSHIP THROUGH PRAYER

In his remarkable sermon "Why Jesus Called a Man a Fool," a weary Martin Luther King Jr. claimed the power of prayer to give buoyancy to the human soul even amid vitriolic complaints and death threats. King confessed,

I bowed down over that cup of coffee—I never will forget it. And oh yes, I prayed a prayer and I prayed out loud that night. I said, "Lord, I'm down here trying to do what's right. I think I'm right; I think the cause that we represent is right. But Lord, I must confess that I'm weak now. I'm faltering; I'm losing courage. And I can't let the people see me like this because if they see me weak and losing my courage, they will begin to get weak. . . ." And it seemed at that moment that I could hear an inner voice saying to me, "Martin Luther, stand up for righteousness, stand up for justice, stand up for truth. And lo I will be with you, even until the end of the world."[28]

King's prayer is reminiscent of Jehoshaphat's prayer as he faced expulsion from the land of promise by the "men of Ammon and Moab and Mount Seir" (2 Chr 20:10). Jehoshaphat, like King, laid his soul bare before God, acknowledging his human ineptness before divine sustainability in confession: "For we are powerless against this great horde that is coming against us. We do not know what to do, but our eyes are on you" (2 Chr 20:12). In prayer, the soul looks to its creator and sustainer and petitions God for our daily bread, the necessities we need to carry out God's will for God's glory. In prophetic radicalism, only through prayer are we able to walk with peace in the face of death and violence and maintain the confident resolve that we are partaking in purposes larger than ourselves.

Prayer's two-way communication of speaking and listening allows for pastors who practice prophetic radicalism to make their requests known but to accept the peace of God's abiding presence when their requests are not granted. Jesus's prayer in the Garden of Gethsemane confirms this truth. Moses's petition to enter the promised land and David's request to build the temple reinforce the fact that peace is better than answered prayer. In prophetic radicalism, sometimes our advocacy for God's redemptive justice falls on deaf ears and hard hearts. However, prayer provides us with the peace and courage we need to remain faithful to the end. Prayer provides rest, and rest restores the weary radical's soul. Barbara L. Peacock provides valuable insight into the partnership of rest and prayer: "The Hebrew word for 'rest' is *nuakh*, which means to be quiet. Another Hebrew word for 'rest' is *shabbat*, meaning to cease. The Greek word for rest is *anapausis*, a call to refreshment. Combining these definitions invites us to a quiet space without struggle that results in a crisp, refreshing season. Oh, what a joyful encounter! Entering God's rest is a call to come away with all aspects of ourselves in the sweet assurance of his presence. Such times are conducive to prayer and encountering God's awesome presence."[29]

The consequences of ignoring the call to rest are severe. The consequences of failing to rest when one is depleted of mental, spiritual, and physical resources lead one to depend on external forces to keep going. Good people may turn to substance abuse with the hope of being empowered to sustain good works. Notice that in the definition of prophetic radicalism, the "acts" we pursue are to be "through the power of the Holy Spirit." God's power is the Holy Spirit, the Giver of life, the Comforter who restores our soul. We access God and God's power through prayer. In speaking of prayer, Jesus reminded his disciples, "If you then, who are evil, know how to give good gifts to your children, how much more will the heavenly Father give the Holy Spirit to those who ask him!" (Luke 11:13).

Conclusion

Radical ministry is demanding because cross-bearing is demanding. Christians are called to carry the cross. Cross-bearing is a sacrificial and selfless service on the behalf of others and in advocacy for our neighbor's community. In this work, weariness is to be expected. Therefore, it is essential that pastors identify the causes of weariness, avoid the self-destructive practices of the messiah complex, and employ the spiritual disciplines of detachment, togetherness, and worship to replenish and restore the soul. The pastor, as a sacred anthropologist engaged in the sacred work of prophetic radicalism, resists the dark forces of evil within the power of the Holy Spirit with a fierce passion and resolve to see humanity liberated from the tyranny of oppression in its varying forms. Rest for the weary radical is as sacred as the work in which they are engaged.

A Final Word

Sacred anthropology *marries prophetic radicalism and the social order for the purpose of affecting a biblically based response designed to call the church to a kingdom focus that holistically addresses humanity.* As such, sacred anthropology is the methodology that empowers pastors and Christians in the pews of churches to do prophetic radicalism. Prophetic radicalism is Christian proclamation *and* living that *expose* the root causes of injustice and *advocate* for God's redemptive justice while *acting* in accord with the life and ministry of Christ through the power of the Holy Spirit. Sacred anthropology sees humanity through the lens of Christ while discerning the complex causes of social crises in our community. Sacred anthropology brings theological anthropology and social-scientific (cultural) anthropology together to provide the church with a methodology to deal prophetically with social injustices in our world.

The work of the sacred anthropologist involves examining historical data, engaging diverse cultures, and immersing oneself in the knowledge of a culture's problems, values, beliefs, and ambitions and even their fears to better understand how to serve them in order to experience spiritual and social liberation in Jesus Christ. The sacred anthropologist interprets all knowledge through the authoritative and divine truths of the Bible, with the presupposition that God wills all of creation to live freely, love deeply, enjoy health and safety, and live out God's redemptive purpose. Prophetic radicalism confronts every challenge to God's purpose for humanity by exposing injustices and advocating for God's redemptive purposes while acting in accord with the life and ministry of Jesus, in the power of the Holy Spirit, to bring God's purposes to pass in the life of every person and community.

Notes

Introduction

1 A fourth painting is of the Underground Railroad.

1. Toward a Theology of Sacred Anthropology

1 Archaeology is the study of material artifacts to understand a culture or society; linguistics involves the study of language; biological anthropology examines human anatomy and human origins.

2 Tanya Maria Golash-Boza, *Race and Racisms: A Critical Approach*, 2nd ed. (New York: Oxford University Press, 2018), 27.

3 For a comprehensive discussion on unwritten rules and staying in the spaces created for them, see Isabel Wilkerson's *Caste: The Origins of Our Discontents* (New York: Random House, 2020).

4 "About AAA—Connect with AAA," American Anthropological Association, accessed January 15, 2022, https://www.americananthro.org/ConnectWithAAA/Content.aspx?ItemNumber=1665&navItemNumber=586.

5 See Mark Charles and Song Chan Rah, *Unsettling Truths: The Ongoing, Dehumanizing Legacy of the Doctrine of Discovery* (Downers Grove, IL: IVP, 2019); chapter 4 of Frank M. Snowden Jr.'s *Before Color Prejudice: The Ancient View of Blacks* (Cambridge, MA: Harvard University Press, 1983); and chapter 7 of Soong-Chan Rah's *The Next Evangelicalism: Freeing the Church from Western Cultural Captivity* (Downers Grove, IL: IVP, 2009).

6 The Southern Baptist Theological Seminary published its "Report on Slavery and Racism in the History of the Southern Baptist Theological Seminary" in late 2018 (https://sbts-wordpress-uploads.s3.amazonaws.com/sbts/uploads/2018/12/Racism-and-the-Legacy-of-Slavery-Report-v4.pdf). This report, conducted by six scholars, testifies to the fact that all the seminary's founding faculty held slaves and defended slaveholding. The seminary's faculty also opposed racial equality. Southern Baptist Theological Seminary's president, Albert Mohler, writes in the introduction of the report, "Many of their successors on this faculty,

throughout the period of Reconstruction and well into the twentieth century, advocated segregation, the inferiority of African Americans, and openly embraced the ideology of the Lost Cause of southern slavery." See especially page 2. For texts that examine flawed hermeneutics and exegetical methodology, see Esau McCaulley, *Reading While Black: African American Biblical Interpretation as an Exercise in Hope* (Downers Grove, IL: IVP Academic, 2020); Lisa M. Bowens, *African American Readings of Paul: Reception, Resistance, and Transformation* (Grand Rapids, MI: Eerdmans, 2020); Mary Beth Swetnam Mathews, *Doctrine and Race: African American Evangelicals and Fundamentalism between the Wars* (Tuscaloosa: University of Alabama Press, 2017); and David M. Goldberg, *The Curse of Ham: Race and Slavery in Early Judaism, Christianity, and Islam* (Princeton, NJ: Princeton University Press, 2003).

7 Malcolm Foley, "Lynching Then and Lynching Now: Racial Justice as Christian Imperative," Mere Orthodoxy, May 7, 2020, https://mereorthodoxy.com/ahmaud -arbery/.

8 Joe R. Feagin, *Systemic Racism: A Theory of Oppression* (New York: Routledge, 2006), xiii.

9 See the Kerner Commission Report of 1968. Originally, the report of the National Advisory Commission on Civil Disorders was a response to Executive Order 11365, issued by President Lyndon Johnson on July 29, 1967. The 426-page report took the name "Kerner Commission Report" from Otto Kerner Jr., then governor of Illinois, who was the chair of the eleven-member commission. The report was the culmination of a seven-month investigation into the riots of 1967 and was to provide recommendations for how the US government could improve race relations in the future. The report also addresses Black life in America and the effects of segregation and other systemic and structural injustices on Black families and communities. Some of the topics in the report include major trends in the Black population, urbanization, white flight, family structure, unemployment, police violence in Black communities, and a host of other social, economic, cultural, and political factors facing African Americans in America's cities. See Jelani Cobb, ed., *The Essential Kerner Commission Report: The Landmark Study on Race, Inequality, and Police Violence* (London: Liveright, 2021); and the National Advisory Commission on Civil Disorders, "Report of the National Advisory Commission on Civil Disorders," accessed January 16, 2022, https://belonging .berkeley.edu/sites/default/files/kerner_commission_full_report.pdf?file=1&force =1, Google Books.

10 Feagin, *Systemic Racism*, 2.

11 Robert Wald Sussman, *The Myth of Race: The Troubling Persistence of an Unscientific Idea* (Cambridge, MA: Harvard University Press, 2014), 2.

12 Brian M. Howell and Jenell William Paris, *Introducing Cultural Anthropology: A Christian Perspective* (Grand Rapids, MI: Baker Academic, 2011), 71.

13 See the American Anthropological Association's "Statement on Race," accessed January 15, 2022, https://www.americananthro.org/ConnectWithAAA/Content .aspx?ItemNumber=2583. For a theologian's view on race and ethnicity, see note 3 in Jarvis J. Williams, *Redemptive Kingdom Diversity: A Biblical Theology of the People of God* (Grand Rapids, MI: Baker Academic, 2021), 12–13.

14 J. Daniel Hays, ed., *From Every People and Nation: A Biblical Theology of Race*, New Studies in Biblical Theology 14 (Downers Grove, IL: InterVarsity, 2003), 141–42.

15 Martin Bulmer and John Solomos, eds., *Racism*, Oxford Readers (Oxford: Oxford University Press, 1999), 8.

16 Harriet A. Washington, *Medical Apartheid: The Dark History of Medical Experimentation on Black Americans from Colonial Times to the Present* (New York: Harlem Moon, 2006), 33.

17 Murray J. Harris, *Slave of Christ: A New Testament Metaphor for Total Devotion to Christ*, New Studies in Biblical Theology 8 (1999; repr., Downers Grove, IL: InterVarsity, 2001), 44.

18 Russell G. Moy, "American Racism: The Null Curriculum in Religious Education," *Religious Education* 95, no. 2 (March 2000): 120, https://doi.org/10.1080/ 0034408000950202.

19 Scientific racism is the employment of anthropology, biology, genetics, psychology, and other scientific disciplines to justify the superiority of one race or ethnicity, usually white, and the inferiority of others, usually non-European. See Tanya Maria Golash-Boza, *Race and Racisms: A Critical Approach*, 3rd ed. (New York: Oxford University Press, 2021); and Angela Saini, *Superior: The Return of Race Science* (London: 4th Estate, 2020). For major nineteenth-century authorities and proponents of scientific racism, see one of the original texts on biological and scientific racism, Arthur de Gobineau's *Essai sur l'inégalité des races humaines [An Essay on the Inequality of the Human Races]* (New York: G. P. Putnam's Sons, 1915); and Josiah C. Nott and George Gliddon's *Types of Mankind: Or Ethnological Researches, Based upon the Ancient Monuments, Paintings, Sculptures, and Crania of Races, and upon Their Natural, Geographical, Philological, and Biblical History* (Philadelphia: Lippincott, Grambo, 1855). See also Samuel George Morton, *An Illustrated System of Human Anatomy: Special, General and Microscopic* (Philadelphia: Grigg, Elliot, 1849); and Samuel George Morton, *Crania Americana: Or a Comparative View of the Skulls of Various Aboriginal Nations of North and South America* (Philadelphia: J. Dobson, 1839).

20 Polygenesis is the theory within scientific racism that held that human races have more than one creator or ancestor. This view was held by some of the leading

scholars, theologians, and philosophers of the seventeenth and eighteenth centuries, including Voltaire, Thomas Jefferson, Rev. James Henley Thornwell, and David Hume. This view of creation was widely used in the defense of slavery. Proponents of slavery, arguing for polygenesis, contended that Africans were different and inferior beings, which legitimized their abuse and enslavement. Proponents of polygenesis also led the way in developing the social construct of race and paved the way for racial hierarchy.

21 This claim is primarily associated with the founders and proponents of critical race theory. For extensive reading on this claim, see Richard Delgado and Jean Stefancic, *Critical Race Theory: The Cutting Edge*, 3rd ed. (Philadelphia: Temple University Press, 2013); Richard Delgado and Jean Stefancic, *Critical Race Theory: An Introduction* (New York: New York University Press, 2017); and Kimberle Crenshaw et al., eds., *Critical Race Theory: The Key Writings That Formed the Movement* (New York: New Press, 1996).

22 For a detailed examination on the historical complicity of the American church regarding racism and racial injustice, see Jemar Tisby, *The Color of Compromise: The Truth about the American Church's Complicity in Racism* (Grand Rapids, MI: Zondervan, 2019).

23 Angela Y. Davis, *Women, Race & Class* (New York: Vintage Books, 1983), 7.

24 *ABC News*, "Alabama Senate Approves Country's Most Restrictive Abortion Ban," May 14, 2019, https://abcnews.go.com/US/alabama-senate-approves-countrys -restrictive-abortion-ban/story?id=63039559.

25 Richard Rothstein, *The Color of Law: A Forgotten History of How Our Government Segregated America* (New York: Liveright, 2017), xii.

26 Alexandra Natapoff, *Punishment without Crime: How Our Massive Misdemeanor System Traps the Innocent and Makes America More Unequal* (New York: Basic Books, 2018), 2.

27 On July 14, 2014, Eric Garner was killed by Daniel Pantaleo, an NYPD officer who used a chokehold to subdue Garner while arresting him on suspicion of selling single cigarettes. Since Garner was not in possession of ten thousand cigarettes or four hundred pounds of tobacco, under NY State Tax Law § 1814, his crime would have been a misdemeanor. Philando Castile was shot by Jeronimo Yanez, a Minneapolis-area police officer, on July 6, 2016, during a traffic stop. Yanez pulled the car, driven by Castile's girlfriend, Diamond Reynolds, over for a broken taillight.

28 See "Children in Adult Prison," Equal Justice Initiative, accessed February 16, 2022, https://eji.org/issues/children-in-prison/#Death_in_Prison_Sentences.

29 See Michelle Alexander, *The New Jim Crow: Mass Incarceration in the Age of Colorblindness* (New York: New Press, 2012); and Reuben Jonathan Miller, *Halfway*

Home: Race, Punishment, and the Afterlife of Mass Incarceration (New York: Little, Brown, 2020).

30 Matthew D. Kim, *Preaching with Cultural Intelligence: Understanding the People Who Hear Our Sermons* (Grand Rapids, MI: Baker Academic, 2017), 3.

2. Prophetic Radicalism

1 Dan McKanan, *Prophetic Encounters: Religion and the American Radical Tradition* (Boston: Beacon, 2011), 2.

2 Jean Calvin, *Calvin: Institutes of the Christian Religion*, ed. John T. McNeill, trans. Ford Lewis Battles, vol. 1 (Philadelphia: Westminster, 1960), 495.

3 Robert Smith Jr., "The Christological Preaching of Helmut Thielicke: The Theocratic Offices as a Paradigm for Preaching" (PhD diss., Southern Baptist Theological Seminary, 1993), 110.

4 The Heidelberg Catechism is a confessional document composed by Zacharias Ursinus in 1563. The Synod of Dort approved the Heidelberg Catechism in 1619, and it remains one of the most celebrated confessions in Reformed Churches.

5 Geoffrey W. Bromiley, *The Evangelical Faith: The Doctrine of God and of Christ*, trans. Helmut Thielicke, vol. 2 (Grand Rapids, MI: Eerdmans, 1982), 358.

6 See James Cone, *God of the Oppressed*, (Maryknoll, NY: Orbis Books, 1975).

7 See Heidelberg Confession, Lord's Day 12, Q & A 31 in *Heidelberg Catechism: Teaching of the Reformed Faith, with Scripture Proofs* (Scotland: ICTHUS, 2016), Kindle.

8 See Heb 5:1; 7:24, 26–27; 2 Chr 15:3; 30:27; Lev 8; 16; 1 Sam 2:22–36; and Joel 2:17.

9 Robin C. McCall, "Holiness Code," in *Dictionary of Scripture and Ethics*, ed. Joel B. Green et al. (Grand Rapids, MI: Baker Academic, 2011), 365.

10 See also Lev 20:26; Mark 1:24; Luke 1:35; Acts 3:14; 4:30; and 2 Cor 5:21.

11 Kent Brower, "Holiness," in Green et al., *Dictionary of Scripture and Ethics*, 363.

12 Brower, 363.

13 Donald W. McCullough, *The Trivialization of God: The Dangerous Illusion of a Manageable Deity* (Colorado Springs: NavPress, 1995), 23.

14 McCall, "Holiness Code," 366.

15 For a detailed investigation into African American Pentecostalism, charismatic churches and denominations, and how their theological beliefs impact racial relationships and respond to social injustice, see Estrelda Y. Alexander, *Black Pentecostalism: One Hundred Years of African American Pentecostalism* (Downers Grove, IL: IVP Academic, 2011).

16 Alexander, 62.

17 McCall, "Holiness Code," 366.

18 Timothy R. Gaines and Kara Lyons-Pardue, eds., *Following Jesus: Prophet, Priest, King* (Kansas City, MO: Foundry, 2018), chap. 2, Kindle.

19 R. Laird Harris, Gleason L. Archer, and Bruce K. Waltke, eds., *Theological Wordbook of the Old Testament* (Chicago: Moody, 1980), 544. See also Exod 7:1; Deut 18:18; 1 Sam 3:20; and Ezek 2:5.

20 See, for example, Jer 1:4; 2:1–2; Ezek 2:7–9; 3:2–3; 3:10; Hos 1:1; Jonah 3:1; and Mic 1:1.

21 Timothy Green, "Following Jesus as Prophet," in Gaines and Lyons-Pardue, *Following Jesus*, chap. 2.

22 Walter Brueggemann, *Hope within History* (Atlanta: Westminster John Knox, 1987), 75.

23 Abraham Joshua Heschel, *The Prophets* (New York: Harper Perennial, 2001), 3.

24 Heschel, 5.

25 Heschel, 4.

26 Scott, *Relevance of the Prophets*, 92.

27 Catherine Clinton, *Harriet Tubman: The Road to Freedom* (New York: Little, Brown, 2004), 27.

28 Stephen B. Oates, *The Fires of Jubilee: Nat Turner's Fierce Rebellion* (New York: HarperCollins, 2009), 35–36, Kindle.

29 Eugene H. Merrill, *Kingdom of Priests: A History of Old Testament Israel*, 2nd ed. (Grand Rapids, MI: Baker Academic, 2008), 293.

30 James H. Harris, *Pastoral Theology: A Black-Church Perspective* (Minneapolis: Fortress, 1991), 5.

3. The Sacred Anthropologist

1 See "Jury Awards $33.5M to Parents of Barstow Man Killed by Deputy," ABC7.com, March 15, 2018, https://abc7.com/barstow-nathaniel-pickett-san -bernardino-county-sheriffs-department-deputy/3220647/.

2 See Sam Levin, "Vallejo Officer Who Shot Willie McCoy Killed Unarmed Man Fleeing on Bike—Video Shows," *Guardian*, May 7, 2019, https://www.theguardian .com/us-news/2019/may/07/vallejo-police-shooting-bike-ronell-foster-willie -mccoy.

3 See "Former Kingsland Police Officer Found Not Guilty of Manslaughter Charges," First Coast News, October 5, 2019, https://www.firstcoastnews .com/article/news/crime/former-kingsland-police-officer-found-not-guilty-of -manslaughter/77-df203c18-39a0-4bb1-83b0-76c2a904f7db.

4 At the time of this writing, six governors have issued bans on teaching critical race theory. See Christopher F. Rufo, "Battle over Critical Race Theory," *Wall Street Journal*, June 27, 2021, https://www.wsj.com/articles/battle-over-critical -race-theory-11624810791; and Jack Dutton, "Critical Race Theory Is Banned in These States," *Newsweek*, June 11, 2021, https://www.msn.com/en-us/news/ us/critical-race-theory-is-banned-in-these-states/ar-AAKWl5g.

5 See "Risk of Severe Illness or Death from COVID-19: Racial and Ethnic Health Disparities," Centers for Disease Control and Prevention, December 10, 2020, https://www.cdc.gov/coronavirus/2019-ncov/community/health-equity/racial -ethnic-disparities/disparities-illness.html.

6 "Rep. Sewell Introduces H.R. 4, the John R. Lewis Voting Rights Advancement Act, to Restore Protections of the Voting Rights Act of 1965," media press release, Congresswoman Terri Sewell Representing Alabama's 7th District, April 17, 2021, https://sewell.house.gov/media-center/press-releases/rep-sewell-introduces -hr-4-john-r-lewis-voting-rights-advancement-act.

7 Miguel A. De La Torre, ed., *Faith and Reckoning after Trump* (Maryknoll, NY: Orbis Books, 2021), 258.

8 "What Is Anthropology," American Anthropological Association, accessed March 9, 2022. https://www.americananthro.org.

9 Sacred anthropology uses cultural anthropology in order to obtain and communicate an understanding of culture from within the culture. This understanding is derived from both common and scholarly voices. For a basic understanding of cultural anthropology as it relates to this study, please see Philip G. Chase, *The Emergence of Culture: The Evolution of a Uniquely Human Way of Life* (New York: Springer, 2006); Gary Ferraro, *Classic Readings in Cultural Anthropology* (Boston: Cengage Learning, 2015); bell hooks, *All about Love: New Visions* (New York: William Morrow, 2001); David I. Kertzer, *Ritual, Politics, and Power* (New Haven, CT: Yale University Press, 1988); Michael G. Kenny and Kirsten Smillie, *Stories of Culture and Place: An Introduction to Anthropology*, 2nd ed. (Toronto: University of Toronto Press, 2017); Kim, *Preaching with Cultural Intelligence*; Charles H. Kraft, *Christianity in Culture: A Study in Biblical Theologizing in Cross-Cultural Perspective* (Maryknoll, NY: Orbis Books, 2005); David A. Livermore, *Cultural Intelligence: Improving Your CQ to Engage Our Multicultural World* (Grand Rapids, MI: Baker Academic, 2009); DeWight R. Middleton, *The Challenge of Human Diversity: Mirrors, Bridges, and Chasms* (Long Grove, IL: Waveland, 2011); Serena Nanda, *Cultural Anthropology*, 12th ed. (Los Angeles: SAGE, 2020); and Snowden Jr., *Before Color Prejudice*.

10 This is not an exhaustive attempt to address the complexities of race and racism. My focus is on how race has harmed the unity of the church. See M. Mathews,

Doctrine and Race; Carolyn Renée Dupont, *Mississippi Praying: Southern White Evangelicals and the Civil Rights Movement, 1945–1975* (New York: New York University Press, 2013); Donald Mathews, *At the Altar of Lynching: Burning Sam Hose in the American South* (Cambridge: Cambridge University Press, 2018); Michael O. Emerson and Christian Smith, *Divided by Faith: Evangelical Religion and the Problem of Race in America* (New York: Oxford University Press, 2001); Richard A. Bailey, *Race and Redemption in Puritan New England* (New York: Oxford University Press, 2014); Rebecca Anne Goetz, *The Baptism of Early Virginia: How Christianity Created Race* (Baltimore: Johns Hopkins University Press, 2016); Tisby, *Color of Compromise*; and J. Russell Hawkins, *The Bible Told Them So: How Southern Evangelicals Fought to Preserve White Supremacy* (New York: Oxford University Press, 2021).

11 Marcus Jerkins, *Black Lives Matter to Jesus: The Salvation of Life and All Life in Luke and Acts* (Minneapolis: Fortress, 2021), 3.

12 Jesse Curtis, *The Myth of Colorblind Christians* (New York: New York University Press, 2021), 206.

13 Jerkins, *Black Lives Matter*, 3.

14 Kelly Brown Douglass, *Resurrection Hope: A Future Where Black Lives Matter* (Maryknoll, NY: Orbis Books, 2021), 160–61.

15 Soon Ang and Linn Van Dyne, "Conceptualization of Cultural Intelligence," in *Handbook of Cultural Intelligence: Theory, Measurement, and Applications*, ed. Soon Ang and Linn Van Dyne (Armonk, NY: M. E. Sharpe, 2008), 3.

16 *Cultural intelligence knowledge* is the understanding one has about cross-cultural issues and differences, while *CQ strategy* is one's willingness to develop an effective strategy to understand and have relationships with other cultures, and *CQ action* asks the question, "How do I need to adapt my behaviors to function effectively on this project?" See David Livermore, *Leading with Cultural Intelligence: The Real Secret to Success* (New York: AMACOM, 2015); and Livermore, *Improving Your CQ*.

17 Livermore, *Leading with Cultural Intelligence*.

18 Emerson and Smith, *Divided by Faith*, 8.

19 Rothstein, *Color of Law*, vii.

20 De La Torre, *Faith and Reckoning after Trump*, 259.

21 Emerson and Smith, *Divided by Faith*, 9.

22 "Health Equity Considerations and Racial and Ethnic Minority Groups," Centers for Disease Control and Prevention, July 2, 2022, https://www.cdc.gov/coronavirus/2019-ncov/community/health-equity/race-ethnicity.html.

23 "Flattened: How the COVID-19 Pandemic Knocked Financially Insecure Alabamians on Their Backs and Widened the Racial Prosperity Gap," Alabama Appleseed Center for Law and Justice, accessed March 12, 2022, https://www

.alabamaappleseed.org/wp-content/uploads/2020/12/Alabama-Appleseed-Covid
-Report-Flattened.pdf.

24 Terence Keel, *Divine Variations: How Christian Thought Became Racial Science* (Stanford, CA: Stanford University Press, 2018), 56–57.

25 Keel, 117.

26 Ta-Nehisi Coates, "The Case for Reparations," *Atlantic*, May 22, 2014, https://www.theatlantic.com/magazine/archive/2014/06/the-case-for-reparations/361631/.

27 Randall Kennedy, *Say It Loud: On Race, Law, History, and Culture* (New York: Pantheon Books, 2021), 24.

28 Frederick Douglass, "What the Black Man Wants," speech at the American Antislavery Society, May 10, 1865, Boston, https://www.lib.rochester.edu/IN/RBSCP/Frederick_Douglass/ATTACHMENTS/Douglass_What_the_Black_Man_Wants.pdf.

29 Duke L. Kwon and Gregory Thompson, *Reparations: A Christian Call for Repentance and Repair* (Grand Rapids, MI: Brazos, 2021), 145.

30 Kwon and Thompson, 21.

31 Rita Omokha, "They Were Sons," *Vanity Fair*, May 6, 2021, https://www.vanityfair.com/news/2021/05/they-were-sons-mothers-of-black-men-killed-by-police-remember-their-losses.

32 See Jordan Guinn, "Officers Cleared in Teen's Slaying," Recordnet.com, July 11, 2012, https://www.recordnet.com/story/news/2012/07/12/officers-cleared-in-teen-s/49565662007/; and Crescenzo Vellucci, "City of Stockton Settles Cop Killing Case with Family for $395,000," Vanguard Sacramento Bureau, December 6, 2019, https://www.davisvanguard.org/2019/12/breaking-news-city-of-stockton-settles-cop-killing-case-with-family-for-395000/.

33 James Cone and Gayraud Wilmore, *Black Theology: A Documentary History, 1966–1979*, vol. 1 (Maryknoll, NY: Orbis Books, 1993), 19–26.

4. Social Crisis Preaching

1 Barry Lee reports on Smith's fame in Nashville by stating, "Smith's move to Nashville led to his ascendancy as the most important Black churchman in Nashville and one of the most dynamic Black Baptist preachers in the country by the 1950s. Smith's church became the nerve center of the Nashville movement while he functioned as the driving force. Therefore, he and First Baptist Church became a force around which the local civil rights movement coalesced." See "The Nashville Civil Rights Movement: A Study of the Phenomenon of Intentional Leadership Development and Its Consequences for Local Movements and the National Civil Rights Movement" (PhD diss., Georgia State University, 2010), 62.

2 Kelly Miller Smith Sr., *Social Crisis Preaching: The Lyman Beecher Lectures 1983* (Macon, GA: Mercer University Press, 1983), 33.

3 Established April 12, 1871, the Lyman Beecher Lectures at Yale Divinity School is one of the most prestigious lecture series on preaching in the nation. At the request of Henry Ward Beecher, the annual lectures were to be named after his father, Lyman Beecher. At the behest of the chief donor, Henry W. Sage, and the Yale Corporation, "the Lyman Beecher lecturer shall be invited to lecture on a branch of pastoral theology or any other topic appropriate to the work of the Christian ministry" ("Bibliography of the Lyman Beecher Lectureship on Preaching," Yale Divinity School, accessed December 12, 2018, https://www .library.yale.edu/div/beecher.html). Among the notables to have delivered these lectures are J. A. Broadus (1888), P. T. Forsyth (1906), John Henry Jowett (1911), Reinhold Niebuhr (1944), Fred Craddock (1977), and Walter Brueggemann (1988). There are also less notable names, but the sermons delivered during the 146 years of the lectures' existence are parallel in substance and scholarship. In 1949, Edgar DeWitt Jones conducted a survey of the Lyman Beecher lecturers, and within that survey he listed several categories, among which is a group that he labels "Prophets of Social Change." The distinguished preachers under that label include Washington Gladden (1886 and 1901), Henry Sloan Coffin (1917), Garfield Bromley Oxman (1943), and Kelly Miller Smith Sr. (1982–83). The other African Americans to preach the Lyman Beecher Lectures are James H. Robinson (1954–55), Henry Mitchell (1973–74), Gardner C. Taylor (1975–76), James Forbes (1985–86), Samuel D. Proctor (1989–90), Thomas Hoyt (1992–93), Peter Gomes (1998), Otis Moss Jr. (2004), Renita J. Weems (the only African American woman; 2008), Brian K. Blount (2011), and Otis Moss III (2014).

4 *Ebony* is the widest circulated magazine of any African American publication in history. Also mentioned in the article are nine of the most notable Black pastors in the United States: Dr. J. H. Jackson, Dr. Miles Mark Fisher, Dr. Benjamin E. Mays, Dr. Mordecai Johnson, Dr. Howard Thurman, Dr. Williams H. Borders, Rev. Adam Clayton Powell Jr., Father Shelton Hale Bishop, and Rev. Archibald J. Carey Jr. "Ten Most Popular Negro Preachers: Ministers Lead Vigorous Public Lives," *Ebony* 9, no. 9 (July 1954): 26–30.

5 My PhD research and dissertation are focused on Kelly Miller Smith Sr. and social crisis preaching. See Anthony Tyshawn Gardner, "An Analysis of Prophetic Radicalism in the Social Crisis Preaching of Kelly Miller Smith, Sr." (PhD diss., Southern Baptist Theological Seminary, 2019). I use James Earl Massey's "radical" component of the five components of African American preaching from his book *The Responsible Pulpit* as a lens to measure the radicality of Smith's

preaching and his concept of social crisis preaching. See James Earl Massey, *The Responsible Pulpit* (Anderson, IN: Warner, 1974).

6 Peter J. Paris, "The Theology and Ministry of Kelly Miller Smith, Sr.: Ecclesiology as a Paradigm for Ministry," *Journal of Religious Thought* 48, no. 1 (Summer/Fall 1991): 6.

7 In one of the most gruesome acts of racial terror, Till had been accused of whistling at Carolyn Bryant, a white woman and the wife of Roy Bryant, his accused murderer and the owner of the store where Mrs. Bryant worked. Mr. Bryant and his half-brother J. W. Milam later beat Till mercilessly, shot him in the back of the head, and tied a cotton gin fan to his lifeless body before throwing him into the Tallahatchie River. Bryant and Milam were acquitted of the murder by an all-white jury. A year later, they confessed to the murder in an interview with *Look* magazine. Kelly Miller Smith was twenty-five at the time of this incident and had assumed the pastorate of First Baptist Church, Capitol Hill, in Nashville.

8 André Resner Jr., ed., *Just Preaching: Prophetic Voices of Economic Justice* (St. Louis: Chalice, 2003), xx.

9 Willem A. VanGemeren, *Interpreting the Prophetic Word: An Introduction to the Prophetic Literature of the Old Testament* (Grand Rapids, MI: Zondervan, 1990), 68.

10 VanGemeren, 27–28.

11 Otis Moss III, *Blue Note Preaching in a Post-soul World: Finding Hope in an Age of Despair* (Louisville, KY: Westminster John Knox, 2015), 15.

12 Walter Brueggemann, *The Practice of Prophetic Imagination: Preaching an Emancipating Word* (Minneapolis: Fortress, 2012), 41.

13 Aristotle, *The Art of Rhetoric*, trans. John Henry Freese (Cambridge, MA: Harvard University Press, 1926), I.ii.7, 17–18.

14 Smith, *Social Crisis Preaching*, 27.

15 Smith, 83.

16 Quintilian, *The Orator's Education*, ed. and trans. D. A. Russell, Loeb Classical Library, vol. 2, bks. 3–5 (Cambridge, MA: Harvard University Press, 2001), 29.

17 Kenyatta R. Gilbert, *A Pursued Justice: Black Preaching from the Great Migration to Civil Rights* (Waco, TX: Baylor University Press, 2016), 5.

18 Smith, *Social Crisis Preaching*, 84.

19 Kelly Miller Smith, "A Look at Ourselves," sermon, Vanderbilt University, Jean and Alexander Heard Library, Special Collections and University Archives, Kelly Miller Smith Papers, box 23, file 13.

20 James Henry Harris, *Black Suffering: Silent Pain, Hidden Hope* (Minneapolis: Fortress, 2020), 164.

21 Cleophus J. LaRue, *The Heart of Black Preaching* (Louisville, KY: Westminster John Knox, 2000), 10.

22 Paul Laurence Dunbar, "Life," in *The Complete Poems of Paul Laurence Dunbar* (New York: Mead, 1922), 8.

23 Langston Hughes, "Mother to Son," in *The Collected Poems of Langston Hughes*, ed. Arnold Rampersad (New York: Vintage Classics, 1994), 30.

24 Joseph Evans, "African American Sacred Rhetoric: An African American Homiletic Style Informed by Western Tradition" (PhD diss., Southern Baptist Theological Seminary, 2005), 12.

25 E. A. Hoffman, "I Must Tell Jesus," in *The New National Baptist Hymnal* (Nashville: National Baptist Publishing Board, 1894), 232.

26 LaRue, *Heart of Black Preaching*, 10.

27 Raymond Bailey, ed., *Hermeneutics for Preaching: Approaches to Contemporary Interpretations of Scripture* (Nashville: Broadman, 1992), 138.

28 Leah D. Schade, "Climate Change Impacts Health, Families, and Wallets," *EcoPreacher* (blog), May 19, 2017, https://www.patheos.com/blogs/ecopreacher/2017/05/climate-change-health-families-wallets/; Leah D. Schade, "EcoPreacher: 'There Will Be Signs': Climate-Crisis Sermon, Advent 1," *EcoPreacher* (blog), November 30, 2015, http://ecopreacher.blogspot.com/2015/11/there-will-be-signs-climate-crisis_30.html.

29 Pastor Rodney Howard Browne is one among many prominent pastors who have insisted that the Covid-19 pandemic is a hoax. Megachurch pastor Kenneth Copeland falsely spread the message that Covid-19 was a strain of the flu. See Jason Wilson, "The Rightwing Christian Preachers in Deep Denial over Covid-19's Danger," *Guardian*, April 4, 2020, https://www.theguardian.com/us-news/2020/apr/04/america-rightwing-christian-preachers-virus-hoax. Churches in Canada have also resisted government warnings. See Robin Willey, "Cash, COVID-19 and Church: How Pandemic Skepticism Is Affecting Religious Communities," Conversation, accessed December 1, 2021, https://theconversation.com/cash-covid-19-and-church-how-pandemic-skepticism-is-affecting-religious-communities-161159.

30 See the CDC's warnings for religious organizations at Centers for Disease Control and Prevention, "CDC 24/7: Saving Lives, Protecting People," accessed May 11, 2022, https://www.cdc.gov/vaccines/covid-19/downloads/best-practices-CBO-FBO.pdf.

31 For an example of sermons that have a high use of interdisciplinary content and meet my definition of social crisis preaching, listen to Gina Stewart's sermon entitled "Jesus Says #MeToo" (Brown Missionary Baptist Church, August 14, 2018, YouTube video, https://www.youtube.com/watch?v=Vd2qDMmNLPE), which addresses the social crisis of sexual abuse. Listen also to my sermon entitled "The Juncture at Joppa" (Beeson Divinity School, Samford

University, September 22, 2020, YouTube video, https://www.youtube.com/watch?v =UEnMJHFd7fs), which challenges cultural supremacy; Charlie Dates's sermon entitled "The Most Segregated Hour in America" (presented at the MLK50 Conference, Memphis, TN, April 3, 2018, YouTube video, https://www.youtube.com/watch?v=9ZT5enPkJA4) exposes racism in the church; and Leah D. Schade's "Beyond 'Creation Care'—Building the Eco-ethical Ark for the Age of Climate Disruption" (presented at the 2018 Luce-Hartford Conference in Christian-Muslim Relations, Hartford, CT, June 18, 2018, YouTube video, https://www .youtube.com/watch?v=D1E606OWoW0) presents an environmental message.

32 Ronald J. Allen, "Preaching on Social Issues," *Encounter* 59, nos. 1–2 (1998): 69, https://www.academia.edu/35269126/PREACHING_ON_SOCIAL_ISSUES.

33 Nikole Hannah-Jones et al., eds., *The 1619 Project: A New Origin Story* (New York: One World, 2021), xvii–xviii.

34 Kelly Miller Smith Sr., "Stay Tuned for Another World," baccalaureate address, June 5, 1966, page 4, Vanderbilt University, Jean and Alexander Heard Library, Special Collections and University Archives, Kelly Miller Smith Papers, box 23, file 4.

35 Martin Luther King Jr., "The Drum Major Instinct," sermon, Ebenezer Baptist Church, February 4, 1968, http://bethlehemfarm.net/wp-content/uploads/2013/02/DrumMajorInstinct.pdf.

36 Prathia Hall, "A Nightmare in Broad Daylight," sermon, Allen Temple Baptist Church, March 29, 1998, https://www.youtube.com/watch?v=PSuC15uLlAA.

37 Forrest E. Harris, *Ministry for Social Crisis: Theology and Praxis in the Black Church Tradition* (Macon, GA: Mercer University Press, 1993), 85.

38 For resources that provide data concerning the US penal system's demographic disparities adversely affecting African American communities, see "Criminal Justice Reform," Equal Justice Initiative, accessed May 11, 2022, https://eji .org/criminal-justice-reform/; "Global Prison Trends 2015," Penal Reform International, accessed May 11, 2022, https://cdn.penalreform.org/wp-content/uploads/2015/04/PRI-Prisons-global-trends-report-LR.pdf; Alexander, *New Jim Crow*; Barry Friedman, *Unwarranted: Policing without Permission* (New York: Farrar, Straus and Giroux, 2017); and Erwin Chemerinsky, *Presumed Guilty: How the Supreme Court Empowered the Police and Subverted Civil Rights* (New York: Liveright, 2021).

39 E. Ann Carson, "Prisoners in 2019," US Department of Justice, Office of Justice Programs, Bureau of Justice Statistics, October 2020, 10, https://bjs.ojp.gov/content/pub/pdf/p19.pdf.

40 The Fugitive Slave Acts were federal laws passed in 1793 and 1850 that allowed for the capture and return of runaway slaves. Black Codes were laws passed by

Southern states after the Civil War that required freed Blacks to show written proof of employment or be fined and/or jailed. Convict leasing allowed state officials to sell the labor of those who were jailed and imprisoned due to the Black Codes to private farms and industries. Convict leasing, another form of slavery, survived based on language in the Thirteenth Amendment that prohibits slavery and involuntary servitude "except as punishment for crime." For the most notable work on the Black Codes and convict leasing, see Douglas A. Blackmon, *Slavery by Another Name: The Re-enslavement of Black Americans from the Civil War to World War II* (New York: Anchor Books, 2008). See also Angela J. Davis, ed., *Policing the Black Man: Arrest, Prosecution, and Imprisonment* (New York: Pantheon, 2017).

41 Smith's obituary, Vanderbilt University, Jean and Alexander Heard Library, Special Collections and University Archives, Kelly Miller Smith Papers, box 16, file 22.

42 Herbert Robinson Marbury, *Pillars of Cloud and Fire: The Politics of Exodus in African American Biblical Interpretation* (New York: New York University Press, 2015), 5.

43 John Britton, "Why Minister Quit $1 Million Baptist Church," *Jet*, January 23, 1964, 25–26. Smith's son, Kelly Miller Smith Jr., also recalls stories of his family's unannounced departure from Antioch Baptist Church on a Sunday morning after his father's sermon. Britton's article in *Jet* includes an interview with Smith with questions focusing on the reason for his return to First Baptist Church, Capitol Hill. Britton states, "At Antioch, Smith presided over 2,670 members. He commanded a $10,000 salary, plus $250 monthly living expenses. A seventeen-year-old credit union at Antioch has assets estimated at over $400,000. The edifice and all its equipment might add up to a half-million dollars, if not more. First Baptist is indeed modest in comparison. It has 450 members, no credit union, and a church valued at about $100,000."

44 Britton, 18.

45 Richard Lischer, *The Preacher King: Martin Luther King Jr. and the Word That Moved America* (New York: Oxford University Press, 1995), 174.

46 Henry H. Mitchell, *Black Preaching: The Recovery of a Powerful Art* (Nashville: Abingdon, 1990), 57.

47 Rhondda Robinson Thomas, *Claiming Exodus: A Cultural History of Afro-Atlantic Identity, 1774–1903* (Waco, TX: Baylor University Press, 2013), 6.

48 Portions of this segment were taken from my PhD dissertation. See Gardner, "Analysis of Prophetic Radicalism."

49 Courtney Pace, *Freedom Faith: The Womanist Vision of Prathia Hall* (Athens: University of Georgia Press, 2019), 1.

50 Keisha N. Blain, *Until I Am Free: Fannie Lou Hamer's Enduring Message to America* (Boston: Beacon, 2021), 44.

51 Blain, 46.

52 Blain, 49.

53 Evelyn Brooks Higginbotham, *Righteous Discontent: The Women's Movement in the Black Baptist Church, 1880–1920* (Cambridge, MA: Harvard University Press, 1994), 3.

54 James Earl Massey, *The Responsible Pulpit* (Anderson, IN: Warner, 1974), chap. 6, Kindle.

55 Leila A. Meier, "'A Different Kind of Prophet': The Role of Kelly Miller Smith in the Nashville Civil Rights Movement, 1955–1960" (master's thesis, Vanderbilt University, 1991), 22.

56 Robert Penn Warren, *Who Speaks for the Negro?* (1965; repr., New Haven, CT: Yale University Press, 2014), 411. See interview manuscripts and hear audio recordings of interviews 1 and 2 at "Kelly Miller Smith," Robert Penn Warren's Who Speaks for the Negro, accessed February 14, 2022, https://whospeaks.library .vanderbilt.edu/interview/kelly-miller-smith.

57 Smith, *Social Crisis Preaching*, 80.

58 Kelly Miller Smith, "The Way of Christ," sermon, Vanderbilt University, Jean and Alexander Heard Library, Special Collections and University Archives, Kelly Miller Smith Papers, box 23, file 4.

59 Kelly Miller Smith, "The Story of Jesus," sermon, Vanderbilt University, Jean and Alexander Heard Library, Special Collections and University Archives, Kelly Miller Smith Papers, box 23, file 4.

60 LaRue, *Heart of Black Preaching*, 88.

61 LaRue, 86.

62 Kelly Miller Smith, "Beauty," sermon, Vanderbilt University, Jean and Alexander Heard Library, Special Collections and University Archives, Kelly Miller Smith Papers, box 23, file 1.

63 Danté Stewart, *Shoutin' in the Fire: An American Epistle* (New York: Convergent, 2021), 66.

5. Old Scars, New Wounds

1 I also use this definition throughout my forthcoming work, *Social Crisis Preaching: Biblical Proclamation for Troubling Times* (Nashville: Broadman Holman Academic, 2022).

2 James P. Hanigan, "Militant Nonviolence: A Spirituality for the Pursuit of Social Justice," *Horizons* 9, no. 1 (1982): 7–22, https://doi.org/10.1017/ S0360966900021927.

3 Philipp Jacob Spener, *Pia Desideria*, trans. Theodore G. Tappert (Eugene, OR: Wipf and Stock, 2002), 105.

4 Willis Jenkins and Jennifer M. McBride, eds., *Bonhoeffer and King: Their Legacies and Import for Christian Social Thought* (Minneapolis: Fortress, 2010), 82.

5 Otis Moss III and Otis Moss Jr., *Preach! The Power and Purpose behind Our Praise* (Cleveland: Pilgrim, 2012), 13.

6 Diana L. Hayes, *Forged in the Fiery Furnace: African American Spirituality* (Maryknoll, NY: Orbis Books, 2012), 3.

7 Hayes, 2.

8 Bryant Myers, "Will the Poor Always Be with Us," Christians for Social Action, April 5, 2018, https://christiansforsocialaction.org/resource/poor-always-with-us/.

9 Hanigan, "Militant Nonviolence," 14.

10 Hanigan, 13.

11 Fort Sumter, near Charleston, South Carolina, is known as the site where the first shots of the Civil War were fired on April 12, 1861, at 4:30 a.m.

12 Matt Schiavenza, "After Charleston's Mass Murder, Forgiveness Duels with Hate," *Atlantic*, June 20, 2015, https://www.theatlantic.com/national/archive/2015/06/Dylann-roof-manifesto-forgiveness/396428/.

13 Peter J. Paris, *The Spirituality of African Peoples: The Search for a Common Moral Discourse* (Minneapolis: Fortress, 1995), 149.

14 Bill Chappell and Richard Gonzales, "Brandt Jean's Act of Grace toward His Brother's Killer Sparks a Debate over Forgiving," NPR, October 3, 2019, National, https://www.npr.org/2019/10/03/766866875/brandt-jeans-act-of-grace-toward-his-brother-s-killer-sparks-a-debate-over-forgi.

15 Martin Luther King Jr., "Nobel Peace Prize Acceptance Speech," University of Oslo, December 10, 1964, https://www.nobelprize.org/prizes/peace/1964/king/acceptance-speech/.

16 Luther D. Ivory, *Toward a Theology of Radical Involvement: The Theological Legacy of Martin Luther King, Jr.* (Nashville: Abingdon, 1997), 71.

17 Timothy P. Jackson, *The Priority of Love: Christian Charity and Social Justice* (Princeton, NJ: Princeton University Press, 2003), 138.

18 Roxane Gay, "Why I Can't Forgive Dylann Roof," *New York Times*, June 23, 2015, Editorial, https://www.nytimes.com/2015/06/24/opinion/why-i-cant-forgive-dylann-roof.html.

19 Jackson, *Priority of Love*, 147.

20 Guyger and her legal team filed the first appeal with the Fifth Circuit Court of Appeals in Dallas, Texas, in August 2021, arguing that Guyger should have been charged with "criminally negligent homicide," which carries a sentence significantly less than the ten years she received for her murder conviction. We should note that in Texas, murder carries a possible penalty of ninety-nine years. The prosecution asked the judge to sentence Guyger to twenty-eight years.

21 Anne Branigin, "What Botham Jean's Mother Had to Say about Dallas Police and Her Son's Show of Forgiveness," The Root, October 4, 2019, https://www.theroot.com/what-botham-jeans-mother-had-to-say-about-dallas-police-1838772274.

22 Fleming Rutledge, *The Crucifixion: Understanding the Death of Jesus Christ* (Grand Rapids, MI: Eerdmans, 2017), 143.

23 Julia Jacobo, "Botham Jean's Mother Delivers Emotional Victim Impact Statement before Sentencing of Amber Guyger: 'My Life Has Not Been the Same,'" ABC News, October 1, 2019, https://abcnews.go.com/US/botham-jeans-mother-delivers-emotional-victim-impact-statement/story?id=65980016.

24 Jackson, *Priority of Love*, 138.

25 Branigin, "Botham Jean's Mother."

26 See, for example, Saint Anselm's *Proslogion*, trans. M. J. Charlesworth (Notre Dame, IN: University of Notre Dame Press, 1979).

27 Rutledge, *Crucifixion*, 115.

28 Jacobo, "Emotional Victim Impact Statement."

29 Jackson, *Priority of Love*, 148.

30 Rutledge, *Crucifixion*, 326.

31 Jackson, *Priority of Love*, 136.

32 J. Harris, *Black Suffering*, 205.

33 Clayborne Carson and Peter Holloran, eds., *A Knock at Midnight: Inspiration from the Great Sermons of Reverend Martin Luther King, Jr.* (New York: Warner Books, 2000), 32.

34 John N. Oswalt, *The Book of Isaiah, Chapters 1–39*, New International Commentary on the Old Testament (Grand Rapids, MI: Eerdmans, 1986), 162.

35 Bruce C. Birch, *Let Justice Roll Down: The Old Testament, Ethics, and Christian Life* (Louisville, KY: Westminster John Knox, 1991), 153.

36 Birch, 123.

37 Darrell L. Bock, *Luke 9:51–24:53*, Baker Exegetical Commentary on the New Testament (Grand Rapids, MI: Baker Academic, 1994), 1451.

38 Ronald J. Allen, Dale P. Andrews, and Dawn Ottoni-Wilhelm, eds., *Preaching God's Transforming Justice: A Lectionary Commentary, Year B* (Louisville, KY: Westminster John Knox, 2011), 20.

39 Howard Thurman, *Deep Is the Hunger: Meditations for Apostles of Sensitiveness* (1951; repr., Richmond, IN: Friends United, 1973).

40 Dallas Willard, *Hearing God: Developing a Conversational Relationship with God* (Downers Grove, IL: IVP, 1984), 20.

41 J. Deotis Roberts, *Bonhoeffer and King: Speaking Truth to Power* (Louisville, KY: Westminster John Knox, 2005), 46.

42 Dietrich Bonhoeffer, *Life Together: The Classic Exploration of Christian Community*, trans. John W. Doberstein (New York: Harper & Row, 1954), 65.

43 Christian T. Collins Winn, "Groaning for the Kingdom of God: Spirituality, Social Justice, and the Witness of the Blumhardts," *Journal of Spiritual Formation and Soul Care* 6, no. 1 (May 2013): 56–75, https://doi.org/10.1177/193979091300600106.

44 John Wimber, *The Dynamics of Spiritual Growth* (London: Hodder & Stoughton, 1991), 196.

45 Carson and Holloran, *Knock at Midnight*, 160–61.

46 Luke Timothy Johnson, *Prophetic Jesus, Prophetic Church: The Challenge of Luke-Acts to Contemporary Christians* (Grand Rapids, MI: Eerdmans, 2011), 44.

47 Johnson, 44.

48 Smith, *Social Crisis Preaching*, 63.

49 Paul R. House, *Old Testament Theology: Twenty Centuries of Unity and Diversity* (Downers Grove, IL: IVP Academic, 1998), 190.

50 Robert M. Franklin, *Crisis in the Village: Restoring Hope in African American Communities* (Minneapolis: Fortress, 2007), 138.

51 Mitchell, *Black Preaching*, 130.

52 LaRue, *Heart of Black Preaching*, 3.

53 Brueggemann, *Practice of Prophetic Imagination*, 4.

54 Joy Turner, "Seeing the Poor and Moving toward Justice: An Interactive Activity," *Social Work & Christianity* 37, no. 2 (Summer 2010): 148, https://www.nacsw.org/member/Publications/49982297.pdf.

55 Willie James Jennings, *Acts*, Belief: A Theological Commentary on the Bible (Louisville, KY: Westminster John Knox, 2017), 39.

56 Saint Basil the Great, *On Social Justice*, trans. C. Paul Schroeder, Popular Patristics, no. 38 (Crestwood, NY: St. Vladimir's Seminary Press, 2009), 70.

57 Søren Kierkegaard, *Works of Love*, trans. Howard Hong and Edna Hong (1847; repr., New York: Harper, 1962), 169.

58 Noel Leo Erskine, *King among the Theologians* (Cleveland: Pilgrim, 1994), 151.

59 Matthew L. Lamb, "Christian Spirituality and Social Justice," *Horizons* 10, no. 1 (1983): 40, https://doi.org/10.1017/S0360966900023331.

60 Hanigan, "Militant Nonviolence," 19.

61 Ivory, *Theology of Radical Involvement*, 170.

6. Sacred Self-Care

1 "President Trump Declares State of Emergency for COVID-19," National Conference of State Legislatures, March 25, 2020, https://www.ncsl.org/ncsl-in-dc/

publications-and-resources/president-trump-declares-state-of-emergency-for
-covid-19.aspx.

2 Mohammed Haddad, "How Many People Have Been Killed by US Police since George Floyd?," Al Jazeera, May 5, 2021, https://www.aljazeera.com/news/2021/ 5/25/how-many-people-have-police-killed-since-george-floyd.

3 This same article states that Black Americans are three times as likely as white Americans to be killed by police.

4 Howard Thurman, *Deep River: Reflections on the Religious Insight of Certain of the Negro Spirituals* (New York: Harper, 1955), 72.

5 Taken from the *Dukes of Hazzard* theme song, "Good Ol' Boys," by Waylon Jennings, 1980.

6 While these closures are often touted as cost-saving measures, evidence of the locations points to voter suppression in poor, majority Black counties. See a glaring example of thirty-one DMV shutdowns in mostly rural Black communities in Susan Watson's article entitled "Alabama's DMV Shutdown Has Everything to Do with Race," ACLU, October 8, 2015, https://www.aclu.org/blog/voting-rights/voting -rights-act/alabamas-dmv-shutdown-has-everything-do-race. For Alabama's voter ID law, see https://www.sos.alabama.gov/alabama-votes/photo-voter-id. During the 2011 Regular Legislative Session, the Legislature approved House Bill 19. Governor Robert Bentley signed the bill, and it was subsequently assigned Act Number 2011-673. However, Vann Newkirk II writes in the *Atlantic*, "In 2015, state Republicans announced the closures of 31 DMV offices across the state, ostensibly in a cost-saving measure. But AL.com journalists Kyle Whitmore and John Archibald found that the closures were concentrated in the black belt, and that of the 10 counties with the highest percentage of nonwhite voters, the state closed DMV offices in eight, and left them without offices entirely, meaning those voters either had to travel long distances to other counties to get licenses or visit special registrar's offices in order to vote." See Vann Newkirk II, "What's Missing from Reports on Alabama's Black Turnout," *Atlantic*, December 7, 2017, https://www.theatlantic.com/politics/ archive/2017/12/can-doug-jones-get-enough-black-voters-to-win/547574/.

7 For further analysis regarding the subject of domination and confronting the powerful structures and systems of violence, I highly recommend Walter Wink, *Engaging the Powers: Discernment and Resistance in a World of Domination* (Minneapolis: Fortress, 1992).

8 Walter Wink, *The Powers That Be: Theology for a New Millennium* (New York: Doubleday, 1999), 82.

9 Alex Van Brunt, "Poor People Rely on Public Defenders Who Are Too Overworked to Defend Them," *Guardian*, June 17, 2015, https://www.theguardian .com/commentisfree/2015/jun/17/poor-rely-public-defenders-too-overworked.

10 "Presumption of Guilt," Equal Justice Initiative, accessed February 16, 2022, https://eji.org/racial-justice/#Presumption_of_Guilt.

11 Joseph Rosenbloom, *Redemption: Martin Luther King Jr.'s Last 31 Hours* (Boston: Beacon, 2018), 1–2.

12 Douglas D. Webster, *Living in Tension: A Theology of Ministry*, vol. 1 (Eugene, OR: Cascade, 2012), 22.

13 Howard Thurman, *The Inward Journey* (Richmond, IN: Friends United, 1961), 112.

14 Barbara L. Peacock, *Soul Care in African American Practice* (Downers Grove, IL: IVP, 2020), 78.

15 Barbara Ann Holmes, *Joy Unspeakable: Contemplative Practices of the Black Church* (Minneapolis: Fortress, 2004), 33.

16 Thurman, *Inward Journey*, 111.

17 Martin Luther King Jr., "Letter from Birmingham Jail," *Christian Century*, June 12, 1963, 767.

18 Dietrich Bonhoeffer, *Life Together*, trans. John W. Doberstein, 5th ed. (Munich: Chr. Kaiser Verlag, 1949), chap. 1, Kindle.

19 Matt 26:38; Rom 12:15; 1 Cor 12:26; Gal 6:2; Phil 4:14.

20 2 Cor 8:1–5; Phil 1:7; 4:14; Col 4:3; 2 Thess 1:4–11.

21 Interview with Danny Steele on Monday, January 3, 2022, Tuscaloosa, AL.

22 Richard J. Foster, *Celebration of Discipline: The Path to Spiritual Growth*, special anniversary ed. (San Francisco: HarperOne, 2018), 160, Kindle.

23 Charles A. Tindley, "Leave It There," hymn, 1916, https://musescore.com/hymns/leave-it-there-charles-a_-tindley.

24 Thurman, *Deep River*, 22–23.

25 Hayes, *Fiery Furnace*, 69.

26 W. E. B. Du Bois, *The Souls of Black Folk* (1903; repr., New York: W. W. Norton, 1999), 157.

27 Hayes, *Fiery Furnace*, 87.

28 Martin Luther King Jr., "Why Jesus Called a Man a Fool," in *Knock at Midnight*, ed. Clayborne Carson and Peter Holloran (New York: Warner Books, 1998), 177, Kindle.

29 Peacock, *Soul Care*, 123.

Selected Bibliography

ABC7.com Staff. "Jury Awards $33.5M to Parents of Barstow Man Killed by Deputy." *ABC7 Los Angeles*, March 16, 2018. https://abc7.com/barstow-nathaniel-pickett -san-bernardino-county-sheriffs-department-deputy/3220647/.

Alexander, Estrelda Y. *Black Fire: One Hundred Years of African American Pentecostalism*. Downers Grove, IL: IVP Academic, 2011.

Alexander, Michelle. *The New Jim Crow: Mass Incarceration in the Age of Colorblindness*. Rev. ed. New York: New Press, 2012.

Allen, Ronald J. "Preaching on Social Issues." *Encounter* 59, nos. 1–2 (1998): 57–76. https://www.academia.edu/35269126/PREACHING_ON_SOCIAL_ISSUES.

Allen, Ronald J., Dale P. Andrews, and Dawn Ottoni-Wilhelm, eds. *Preaching God's Transforming Justice: A Lectionary Commentary, Year B*. Louisville, KY: Westminster John Knox, 2011.

AME Church. "Our Beliefs." Accessed January 16, 2022. https://www.ame-church .com/our-church/our-beliefs/.

American Anthropological Association. "AAA Statement on Race—Connect with AAA." Accessed January 15, 2022. https://www.americananthro.org/ ConnectWithAAA/Content.aspx?ItemNumber=2583.

———. "About AAA—Connect with AAA." Accessed January 15, 2022. https://www .americananthro.org/ConnectWithAAA/Content.aspx?ItemNumber=1665& navItemNumber=586.

Bailey, Richard A. *Race and Redemption in Puritan New England*. New York: Oxford University Press, 2011.

Bantu, Vince L. *A Multitude of All Peoples: Engaging Ancient Christianity's Global Identity*. Missiological Engagements Series. Downers Grove, IL: IVP Academic, 2020.

Beecher, Lyman. *A Plea for the West*. 1835. Reprint, Miami: HardPress, 2017. Kindle.

Birch, Bruce C. *Let Justice Roll Down: The Old Testament, Ethics, and Christian Life*. Louisville, KY: Westminster John Knox, 1991.

Blackmon, Douglas A. *Slavery by Another Name: The Re-enslavement of Black Americans from the Civil War to World War II*. New York: Doubleday, 2009.

Blain, Keisha N. *Until I Am Free: Fannie Lou Hamer's Enduring Message to America*. Boston: Beacon, 2021.

Bock, Darrell L. *Luke 9:51–24:53*. Baker Exegetical Commentary on the New Testament 3. Grand Rapids, MI: Baker Academic, 1994.

Bonhoeffer, Dietrich. *Life Together: The Classic Exploration of Christian Community*. Translated by John W. Doberstein. New York: Harper & Row, 1954.

Bowens, Lisa M. *African American Readings of Paul: Reception, Resistance, and Transformation*. Grand Rapids, MI: Eerdmans, 2020.

Branigin, Anne. "What Botham Jean's Mother Had to Say about Dallas Police and Her Son's Show of Forgiveness." The Root, October 4, 2019. https://www.theroot.com/what-botham-jeans-mother-had-to-say-about-dallas-police-1838772274.

Britton, John. "Why Minister Quit $1 Million Baptist Church." *Jet*, January 23, 1964.

Brown, Sally A. *Sunday's Sermon for Monday's World: Preaching to Shape Daring Witness*. The Gospel and Our Culture. Grand Rapids, MI: Eerdmans, 2020.

Brueggemann, Walter. *The Practice of Prophetic Imagination: Preaching an Emancipating Word*. Minneapolis: Fortress, 2012.

Bulmer, Martin, and John Solomos, eds. *Racism*. Oxford Readers. Oxford: Oxford University Press, 1999.

Calvin, Jean. *Calvin: Institutes of the Christian Religion*. Edited by John T. McNeill. Translated by Ford Lewis Battles. Vol. 1. Philadelphia: Westminster, 1960.

Carson, Clayborne, and Peter Holloran, eds. *A Knock at Midnight: Inspiration from the Great Sermons of Reverend Martin Luther King, Jr.* New York: Warner Books, 2000.

Carson, E. Ann. "Prisoners in 2019." US Department of Justice, Office of Justice Programs, Bureau of Justice Statistics, October 2020. https://bjs.ojp.gov/content/pub/pdf/p19.pdf.

Centers for Disease Control and Prevention. "Risk of Severe Illness or Death from COVID-19: Racial and Ethnic Health Disparities." December 10, 2020. https://www.cdc.gov/coronavirus/2019-ncov/community/health-equity/racial-ethnic-disparities/disparities-illness.html.

Chappell, Bill, and Richard Gonzales. "Brandt Jean's Act of Grace toward His Brother's Killer Sparks a Debate over Forgiving." National. NPR, October 3, 2019. https://www.npr.org/2019/10/03/766866875/brandt-jeans-act-of-grace-toward-his-brother-s-killer-sparks-a-debate-over-forgi.

Charles, Mark, and Soong-Chan Rah. *Unsettling Truths: The Ongoing, Dehumanizing Legacy of the Doctrine of Discovery*. Downers Grove, IL: IVP, 2019.

Chemerinsky, Erwin. *Presumed Guilty: How the Supreme Court Empowered the Police and Subverted Civil Rights*. New York: Liveright, 2021.

Cilluffo, Anthony, and D'Vera Cohn. "6 Demographic Trends Shaping the U.S. and the World in 2019." *Pew Research Center* (blog), accessed January 16, 2022. https://www.pewresearch.org/fact-tank/2019/04/11/6-demographic-trends-shaping-the-u-s-and-the-world-in-2019/.

Clinton, Catherine. *Harriet Tubman: The Road to Freedom.* New York: Little, Brown, 2005.

Coates, Ta-Nehisi. "The Case for Reparations." *Atlantic*, May 22, 2014. https://www
.theatlantic.com/magazine/archive/2014/06/the-case-for-reparations/361631/.

Collins Winn, Christian T. "Groaning for the Kingdom of God: Spirituality, Social
Justice, and the Witness of the Blumhardts." *Journal of Spiritual Formation and Soul
Care* 6, no. 1 (May 2013): 56–75. https://doi.org/10.1177/193979091300600106.

Dabney, Robert Lewis. *A Defence of Virginia: (And through Her, of the South) in Recent and
Pending Contests against the Sectional Party.* New York: E. J. Hale, 1867.

Dates, Charlie. "The Most Segregated Hour in America." Presented at the MLK50
Conference, Memphis, TN, April 3, 2018. YouTube video. https://www.youtube
.com/watch?v=9ZT5enPkJA4.

Davis, Angela J., ed. *Policing the Black Man: Arrest, Prosecution, and Imprisonment.* New
York: Pantheon, 2017.

Douglas, Kelly Brown. *Stand Your Ground: Black Bodies and the Justice of God.* Maryknoll,
NY: Orbis Books, 2015.

Douglass, Frederick. *Narrative of the Life of Frederick Douglass, an American Slave.* 1845.
Reprint, New York: Barnes & Noble, 2003.

Du Bois, W. E. B. *The Souls of Black Folk.* Norton Critical Editions. 1903. Reprint, New
York: W. W. Norton, 1999.

Dunbar, Paul Laurence. "Life." Poets.org, accessed January 17, 2022. https://poets
.org/poem/life-5.

Dupont, Carolyn Renée. *Mississippi Praying: Southern White Evangelicals and the Civil
Rights Movement, 1945–1975.* New York: New York University Press, 2013.

Dutton, Jack. "Critical Race Theory Is Banned in These States." *Newsweek*, June 11,
2021. https://www.newsweek.com/critical-race-theory-banned-these-states
-1599712.

Ebony. "Ten Most Popular Negro Preachers: Ministers Lead Vigorous Public Lives."
July 1954.

Edwards, O. C. *A History of Preaching.* Nashville: Abingdon, 2016. Kindle.

Emerson, Michael O., and Christian Smith. *Divided by Faith: Evangelical Religion and
the Problem of Race in America.* Oxford: Oxford University Press, 2001.

Equal Justice Initiative. "Children in Adult Prison." Accessed January 15, 2022. https://
eji.org/issues/children-in-prison/.

———. "Criminal Justice Reform." Accessed January 16, 2022. https://eji.org/criminal
-justice-reform/.

Erskine, Noel Leo. *King among the Theologians.* Cleveland: Pilgrim, 1994.

Evans, Joseph. "African American Sacred Rhetoric: An African American Homiletic
Style Informed by Western Tradition." PhD diss., Southern Baptist Theological
Seminary, 2005.

Feagin, Joe R. *Systemic Racism: A Theory of Oppression*. New York: Routledge, 2006.

Felder, Cain Hope, ed. *Stony the Road We Trod: African American Biblical Interpretation*. Minneapolis: Fortress, 1991.

First Coast News. "Former Kingsland Police Officer Found Not Guilty of Manslaughter Charges." 12news.com, October 3, 2019. https://www.12news.com/article/news/crime/former-kingsland-police-officer-found-not-guilty-of-manslaughter/77-df203c18-39a0-4bb1-83b0-76c2a904f7db.

Foster, Richard J. *Celebration of Discipline: The Path to Spiritual Growth*. Special anniversary ed. San Francisco: HarperOne, 2018. Kindle.

Franklin, Robert Michael. *Crisis in the Village: Restoring Hope in African American Communities*. Minneapolis: Fortress, 2007.

Friedman, Barry. *Unwarranted: Policing without Permission*. New York: Farrar, Straus and Giroux, 2017.

Gardner, Tyshawn. "The Juncture at Joppa." Beeson Divinity School, Samford University, September 22, 2020. YouTube video. https://www.youtube.com/watch?v=UEnMJHFd7fs.

Gay, Roxane. "Why I Can't Forgive Dylann Roof." Editorial. *New York Times*, June 23, 2015. https://www.nytimes.com/2015/06/24/opinion/why-i-cant-forgive-dylann-roof.html.

Gilbert, Kenyatta R. *A Pursued Justice: Black Preaching from the Great Migration to Civil Rights*. Waco, TX: Baylor University Press, 2016.

Goetz, Rebecca Anne. *The Baptism of Early Virginia: How Christianity Created Race*. Baltimore: Johns Hopkins University Press, 2016.

Golash-Boza, Tanya Maria. *Race and Racisms: A Critical Approach*. 2nd ed. New York: Oxford University Press, 2018.

Goldenberg, David M. *The Curse of Ham: Race and Slavery in Early Judaism, Christianity, and Islam*. Princeton, NJ: Princeton University Press, 2003.

Green, Joel B., Jacqueline E. Lapsley, Rebekah Miles, and Allen Verhey, eds. *Dictionary of Scripture and Ethics*. Grand Rapids, MI: Baker Academic, 2011.

Green, Timothy. "Following Jesus as Prophet." In *Following Jesus: Prophet, Priest, King*, edited by Timothy R. Gaines and Kara Lyons-Pardue, chap. 2. Kansas City, MO: Foundry, 2018. Kindle.

Haddad, Mohammed. "How Many People Have Been Killed by US Police since George Floyd?" Al Jazeera, May 5, 2021. https://www.aljazeera.com/news/2021/5/25/how-many-people-have-police-killed-since-george-floyd.

Hall, Prathia. "A Nightmare in Broad Daylight." Sermon, Allen Temple Baptist Church, March 29, 1998. YouTube video. https://www.youtube.com/watch?v=PSuC15uLlAA.

Hanigan, James P. "Militant Nonviolence: A Spirituality for the Pursuit of Social Justice." *Horizons* 9, no. 1 (1982): 7–22. https://doi.org/10.1017/S03609669000 21927.

Hannah-Jones, Nikole, Caitlin Roper, Ilana Silverman, and Jake Silverstein, eds. *The 1619 Project: A New Origin Story*. New York: One World, 2021.

Harris, Forrest E. *Ministry for Social Crisis: Theology and Praxis in the Black Church Tradition*. Macon, GA: Mercer University Press, 1993.

Harris, James Henry. *Black Suffering: Silent Pain, Hidden Hope*. Minneapolis: Fortress, 2020.

———. *Pastoral Theology: A Black-Church Perspective*. Minneapolis: Fortress, 1991.

Harris, Murray J. *Slave of Christ: A New Testament Metaphor for Total Devotion to Christ*. New Studies in Biblical Theology 8. 1999. Reprint, Downers Grove, IL: InterVarsity, 2001.

Harris, R. Laird, Gleason L. Archer, and Bruce K. Waltke, eds. *Theological Wordbook of the Old Testament*. Chicago: Moody, 1980.

Hatcher, William E. *John Jasper: The Unmatched Negro Philosopher and Preacher*. New York: Negro Universities Press, 1969.

Hawkins, J. Russell. *The Bible Told Them So: How Southern Evangelicals Fought to Preserve White Supremacy*. New York: Oxford University Press, 2021.

Hayes, Diana L. *Forged in the Fiery Furnace: African American Spirituality*. Maryknoll, NY: Orbis Books, 2012.

Hays, J. Daniel, ed. *From Every People and Nation: A Biblical Theology of Race*. New Studies in Biblical Theology 14. Downers Grove, IL: InterVarsity, 2003.

Heschel, Abraham Joshua. *The Prophets*. New York: Harper Perennial, 2001.

Higginbotham, Evelyn Brooks. *Righteous Discontent: The Women's Movement in the Black Baptist Church, 1880–1920*. Cambridge, MA: Harvard University Press, 1994.

Holmes, Barbara Ann. *Joy Unspeakable: Contemplative Practices of the Black Church*. Minneapolis: Fortress, 2004.

House, Paul R. *Old Testament Theology: Twenty Centuries of Unity and Diversity*. Downers Grove, IL: IVP Academic, 1998.

Howell, Brian M., and Jenell Williams Paris. *Introducing Cultural Anthropology: A Christian Perspective*. Grand Rapids, MI: Baker Academic, 2011.

Hughes, Langston. "Mother to Son." Poets.org, accessed January 17, 2022. https:// poets.org/poem/mother-son.

Ivory, Luther D. *Toward a Theology of Radical Involvement: The Theological Legacy of Martin Luther King, Jr.* Nashville: Abingdon, 1997.

Jackson, Timothy Patrick. *The Priority of Love: Christian Charity and Social Justice*. New Forum Books. Princeton, NJ: Princeton University Press, 2003.

Jacobo, Julia. "Botham Jean's Mother Delivers Emotional Victim Impact Statement before Sentencing of Amber Guyger: 'My Life Has Not Been the Same.'" ABC News, October 1, 2019. https://abcnews.go.com/US/botham-jeans-mother-delivers -emotional-victim-impact-statement/story?id=65980016.

Jenkins, Willis, and Jennifer M. McBride, eds. *Bonhoeffer and King: Their Legacies and Import for Christian Social Thought*. Minneapolis: Fortress, 2010.

Jennings, Willie James. *Acts*. Belief: A Theological Commentary on the Bible. Louisville, KY: Westminster John Knox, 2017.

Johnson, Luke Timothy. *Prophetic Jesus, Prophetic Church: The Challenge of Luke-Acts to Contemporary Christians*. Grand Rapids, MI: Eerdmans, 2011.

Kidd, Colin. *The Forging of Races: Race and Scripture in the Protestant Atlantic World, 1600–2000*. Cambridge: Cambridge University Press, 2006. Kindle.

Kierkegaard, Søren. *Works of Love*. Translated by Howard Hong and Edna Hong. 1847. Reprint, New York: Harper, 1962.

Kim, Matthew D. *Preaching with Cultural Intelligence: Understanding the People Who Hear Our Sermons*. Grand Rapids, MI: Baker Academic, 2017.

King, Martin Luther, Jr. "The Drum Major Instinct." Sermon, Ebenezer Baptist Church, February 4, 1968. http://bethlehemfarm.net/wp-content/uploads/2013/ 02/DrumMajorInstinct.pdf.

———. "Letter from Birmingham Jail." *Christian Century*, June 12, 1963.

———. "Nobel Peace Prize Acceptance Speech." University of Oslo, December 10, 1964. https://www.nobelprize.org/prizes/peace/1964/king/acceptance-speech/.

Lamb, Matthew L. "Christian Spirituality and Social Justice." *Horizons* 10, no. 1 (1983): 32–49. https://doi.org/10.1017/S0360966900023331.

LaRue, Cleophus J. *The Heart of Black Preaching*. Louisville, KY: Westminster John Knox, 2000.

Lee, Barry. "The Nashville Civil Rights Movement: A Study of the Phenomenon of Intentional Leadership Development and Its Consequences for Local Movements and the National Civil Rights Movement." PhD diss., Georgia State University, 2010.

Levin, Sam. "Vallejo Officer Who Shot Willie McCoy Killed Unarmed Man Fleeing on Bike—Video Shows." US News. *Guardian*, May 7, 2019. https://www.theguardian .com/us-news/2019/may/07/vallejo-police-shooting-bike-ronell-foster-willie-mccoy.

Lincoln, C. Eric, and Lawrence H. Mamiya. *The Black Church in the African-American Experience*. Durham, NC: Duke University Press, 1990.

Lischer, Richard. *The Preacher King: Martin Luther King Jr. and the Word That Moved America*. New York: Oxford University Press, 1995.

Marbury, Herbert Robinson. *Pillars of Cloud and Fire: The Politics of Exodus in African American Biblical Interpretation*. Religion and Social Transformation. New York: New York University Press, 2015.

Massey, James Earl. *The Responsible Pulpit*. 1974. Reprint, Minneapolis: Fleming Services, 2018. Kindle.

Mather, Cotton. *The Negro Christianized: An Essay to Excite and Assist That Good Work, the Instruction of Negro-Servants in Christianity*. Boston: Green, 1706.

Mathews, Donald G. *At the Altar of Lynching: Burning Sam Hose in the American South*. Cambridge Studies on the American South. New York: Cambridge University Press, 2018.

Mathews, Mary Beth Swetnam. *Doctrine and Race: African American Evangelicals and Fundamentalism between the Wars*. Tuscaloosa: University of Alabama Press, 2018.

McCaulley, Esau. *Reading While Black: African American Biblical Interpretation as an Exercise in Hope*. Downers Grove, IL: IVP Academic, 2020.

McCullough, Donald W. *The Trivialization of God: The Dangerous Illusion of a Manageable Deity*. Colorado Springs: NavPress, 1995.

McKanan, Dan. *Prophetic Encounters: Religion and the American Radical Tradition*. Boston: Beacon, 2011.

Meier, Leila A. "'A Different Kind of Prophet': The Role of Kelly Miller Smith in the Nashville Civil Rights Movement, 1955–1960." Master's thesis, Vanderbilt University, 1991.

Merrill, Eugene H. *Kingdom of Priests: A History of Old Testament Israel*. 2nd ed. Grand Rapids, MI: Baker Academic, 2008.

Miller, Reuben Jonathan. *Halfway Home: Race, Punishment, and the Afterlife of Mass Incarceration*. New York: Little, Brown, 2021.

Mitchell, Henry H. *Black Preaching: The Recovery of a Powerful Art*. Nashville: Abingdon, 1990.

Moody Bible Institute. *Founder's Week 2019 Charlie Dates*. February 6, 2019. YouTube video. https://www.youtube.com/watch?v=hmLe_1bKK2o.

Morton, Samuel George. *Crania Americana: Or a Comparative View of the Skulls of Various Aboriginal Nations of North and South America*. 1839. Reprint, London: Forgotten Books, 2012.

———. *An Illustrated System of Human Anatomy: Special, General and Microscopic*. 1849. Reprint, London: Forgotten Books, 2018.

Moss, Otis, III. *Blue Note Preaching in a Post-soul World: Finding Hope in an Age of Despair*. Louisville, KY: Westminster John Knox, 2015.

Moss, Otis, III, and Otis Moss Jr. *Preach! The Power and Purpose behind Our Praise*. Cleveland: Pilgrim, 2012.

Moy, Russell G. "American Racism: The Null Curriculum in Religious Education." *Religious Education* 95, no. 2 (March 2000): 119–133. https://doi.org/10.1080/0034408000950202.

Natapoff, Alexandra. *Punishment without Crime: How Our Massive Misdemeanor System Traps the Innocent and Makes America More Unequal*. New York: Basic Books, 2018.

National Conference of State Legislatures. "President Trump Declares State of Emergency for COVID-19." March 25, 2020. https://www.ncsl.org/ncsl-in-dc/publications-and-resources/president-trump-declares-state-of-emergency-for-covid-19.aspx.

Nott, Josiah C., and George R. Gliddon. *Types of Mankind*. Philadelphia: J. B. Lippincott, 1857.

Oates, Stephen B. *The Fires of Jubilee: Nat Turner's Fierce Rebellion*. New York: Harper Collins, 2009. Kindle.

Oden, Thomas C. *How Africa Shaped the Christian Mind: Rediscovering the African Seedbed of Western Christianity*. Downers Grove, IL: InterVarsity, 2007.

Oswalt, John N. *The Book of Isaiah, Chapters 1–39*. New International Commentary on the Old Testament. Grand Rapids, MI: Eerdmans, 1986.

Pace, Courtney. *Freedom Faith: The Womanist Vision of Prathia Hall*. Athens: University of Georgia Press, 2019.

Paris, Peter J. *The Spirituality of African Peoples: The Search for a Common Moral Discourse*. Minneapolis: Fortress, 1994.

———. "The Theology and Ministry of Kelly Miller Smith, Sr.: Ecclesiology as a Paradigm for Ministry." *Journal of Religious Thought* 48, no. 1 (Summer/Fall 1991): 5–19.

Peacock, Barbara L. *Soul Care in African American Practice*. Downers Grove, IL: IVP, 2020.

Quintilian. *The Orator's Education*. Translated by D. A. Russell. Loeb Classical Library. Vol. 2, bks. 3–5. Cambridge, MA: Harvard University Press, 2001.

Raboteau, Albert J. *Slave Religion: The "Invisible Institution" in the Antebellum South*. Oxford: Oxford University Press, 2004.

Rah, Soong-Chan. *The Next Evangelicalism: Freeing the Church from Western Cultural Captivity*. Downers Grove, IL: IVP, 2009.

Roberts, J. Deotis. *Bonhoeffer and King: Speaking Truth to Power*. Louisville, KY: Westminster John Knox, 2005.

Robertson, E. H. *Dietrich Bonhoeffer*. London: Westminster John Knox, 1966.

Rodríguez, Rubén Rosario. "Dispatches from the Deep State: The Political Theology of QAnon." In *Faith and Reckoning after Trump*, edited by Miguel A. De La Torre, 25–35. Maryknoll, NY: Orbis Books, 2021.

Rosenbloom, Joseph. *Redemption: Martin Luther King Jr.'s Last 31 Hours*. Boston: Beacon, 2018.

Rothstein, Richard. *The Color of Law: A Forgotten History of How Our Government Segregated America*. 1st ed. New York: Liveright, 2017.

Rufo, Christopher F. "Battle over Critical Race Theory." Editorial. *Wall Street Journal*, June 27, 2021. https://www.wsj.com/articles/battle-over-critical-race-theory-11624810791.

Rutledge, Fleming. *The Crucifixion: Understanding the Death of Jesus Christ*. Grand Rapids, MI: Eerdmans, 2017.

Saini, Angela. *Superior: The Return of Race Science*. Boston: Beacon, 2019.

Saint Anselm. *St. Anselm's Proslogion with a Reply on Behalf of the Fool by Gaunilo and the Author's Reply to Gaunilo*. Translated by M. J. Charlesworth. 1078. Reprint, Notre Dame, IN: University of Notre Dame Press, 1979.

Saint Basil the Great. *On Social Justice*. Translated by C. Paul Schroeder. Popular Patristics, no. 38. Crestwood, NY: St. Vladimir's Seminary Press, 2009.

Sanneh, Lamin O. *Whose Religion Is Christianity? The Gospel beyond the West*. Grand Rapids, MI: Eerdmans, 2003.

Schade, Leah D. "Beyond 'Creation Care'—Building the Eco-ethical Ark for the Age of Climate Disruption." Presented at the 2018 Luce-Hartford Conference in Christian-Muslim Relations, Hartford, CT, June 18, 2018. YouTube video. https://www.youtube.com/watch?v=D1E606OWoW0.

———. "Climate Change Impacts Health, Families, and Wallets." *EcoPreacher* (blog), May 19, 2017. https://www.patheos.com/blogs/ecopreacher/2017/05/climate-change-health-families-wallets/.

———. "'There Will Be Signs': Climate-Crisis Sermon, Advent 1." *EcoPreacher* (blog), November 30, 2015. http://ecopreacher.blogspot.com/2015/11/there-will-be-signs-climate-crisis_30.html.

Schiavenza, Matt. "After Charleston's Mass Murder, Forgiveness Duels with Hate." *Atlantic*, June 20, 2015. https://www.theatlantic.com/national/archive/2015/06/dylann-roof-manifesto-forgiveness/396428/.

Scott, R. B. Y. *The Relevance of the Prophets: An Introduction to the Old Testament Prophets and Their Message*. New York: Macmillan, 1944.

Smith, Kelly Miller, Sr. Kelly Miller Smith Papers. Jean and Alexander Heard Library, Special Collections and University Archives, Vanderbilt University, Nashville, TN.

———. *Social Crisis Preaching: The Lyman Beecher Lectures 1983*. Macon, GA: Mercer University Press, 1987.

Smith, Robert, Jr. "The Christological Preaching of Helmut Thielicke: The Theocratic Offices as a Paradigm for Preaching." PhD diss., Southern Baptist Theological Seminary, 1993.

Snowden, Frank M. *Before Color Prejudice: The Ancient View of Blacks*. Cambridge, MA: Harvard University Press, 1991.

Southern Baptist Theological Seminary. "Report on Slavery and Racism in the History of the Southern Baptist Theological Seminary." December 2018. https://sbts

-wordpress-uploads.s3.amazonaws.com/sbts/uploads/2018/12/Racism-and-the
-Legacy-of-Slavery-Report-v4.pdf.

Spener, Philipp Jacob. *Pia Desideria*. Translated by Theodore G. Tappert. Reprint, Eugene, OR: Wipf and Stock, 2002.

Stewart, Danté. *Shoutin' in the Fire: An American Epistle*. New York: Convergent, 2021.

Stewart, Gina. "Jesus Says #MeToo." Brown Missionary Baptist Church, August 14, 2018. YouTube video. https://www.youtube.com/watch?v=Vd2qDMmNLPE.

Sussman, Robert W. *The Myth of Race: The Troubling Persistence of an Unscientific Idea*. Cambridge, MA: Harvard University Press, 2014.

Thomas, Rhondda Robinson. *Claiming Exodus: A Cultural History of Afro-Atlantic Identity, 1774–1903*. Waco, TX: Baylor University Press, 2013.

Thurman, Howard. *Deep Is the Hunger: Meditations for Apostles of Sensitiveness*. 1951. Reprint, Richmond, IN: Friends United, 1973.

———. *Deep River: Reflections on the Religious Insight of Certain of the Negro Spirituals*. New York: Harper, 1955.

———. *The Inward Journey*. Richmond, IN: Friends United, 1961.

———. *Jesus and the Disinherited*. 1949. Reprint, Boston: Beacon, 2022.

Tisby, Jemar. *The Color of Compromise: The Truth about the American Church's Complicity in Racism*. Grand Rapids, MI: Zondervan, 2019.

Turner, Joy. "Seeing the Poor and Moving toward Justice: An Interactive Activity." *Social Work & Christianity* 37, no. 2 (Summer 2010): 142–160. https://www.nacsw.org/member/Publications/49982297.pdf.

VanGemeren, Willem. *Interpreting the Prophetic Word: An Introduction to the Prophetic Literature of the Old Testament*. Grand Rapids, MI: Zondervan, 1990.

Warren, Robert Penn. *Who Speaks for the Negro?* 1965. Reprint, New Haven, CT: Yale University Press, 2014.

Washington, Harriet A. *Medical Apartheid: The Dark History of Medical Experimentation on Black Americans from Colonial Times to the Present*. New York: Harlem Moon, 2006.

Webster, Douglas D. *Living in Tension: A Theology of Ministry*. Vol. 1. 2 vols. Eugene, OR: Cascade, 2012.

White, Wesley W. "Incorporating Perspectives from the African-American Homiletic Tradition in Order to Increase Socio-political Awareness and Activism among Evangelicals." Denver: Denver Seminary, 2000.

Wilhite, David E. *Ancient African Christianity: An Introduction to a Unique Context and Tradition*. London: Routledge, 2017.

Wilkerson, Isabel. *Caste: The Origins of Our Discontents*. New York: Random House, 2020.

Willard, Dallas. *Hearing God: Developing a Conversational Relationship with God*. Downers Grove, IL: IVP, 1984.

Willey, Robin. "Cash, COVID-19 and Church: How Pandemic Skepticism Is Affecting Religious Communities." Conversation, accessed January 17, 2022. http:// theconversation.com/cash-covid-19-and-church-how-pandemic-skepticism-is -affecting-religious-communities-161159.

Williams, Jarvis J. *Redemptive Kingdom Diversity: A Biblical Theology of the People of God.* Grand Rapids, MI: Baker Academic, 2021.

Wills, Gregory A. *Southern Baptist Theological Seminary, 1859–2009.* Oxford: Oxford University Press, 2009.

Wilson, Jason. "The Rightwing Christian Preachers in Deep Denial over Covid-19's Danger." US News. *Guardian*, April 4, 2020. https://www.theguardian.com/us -news/2020/apr/04/america-rightwing-christian-preachers-virus-hoax.

Wimber, John. *The Dynamics of Spiritual Growth.* London: Hodder & Stoughton, 1991.

Wink, Walter. *Engaging the Powers: Discernment and Resistance in a World of Domination.* Powers 3. Minneapolis: Fortress, 1992.

———. *The Powers That Be: Theology for a New Millennium.* New York: Doubleday, 1999.

General Index

Scripture Index